LUSH&LAYERED
beadweaving
STITCH JEWELRY WITH TEXTURE AND DIMENSION

Marcia Balonis

KALMBACH BOOKS

WAUKESHA, WISCONSIN

Kalmbach Books
21027 Crossroads Circle
Waukesha, Wisconsin 53186
www.JewelryAndBeadingStore.com

Published in 2018
22 21 20 19 18   2 3 4 5 6

Manufactured in China

ISBN: 978-1-62700-453-4
EISBN: 978-1-62700-454-1

Editor: Erica Barse
Technical Editor: Jane Danley Cruz
Book Design: Lisa Bergman
Photographer: William Zuback

Library of Congress Control Number: 2017934277

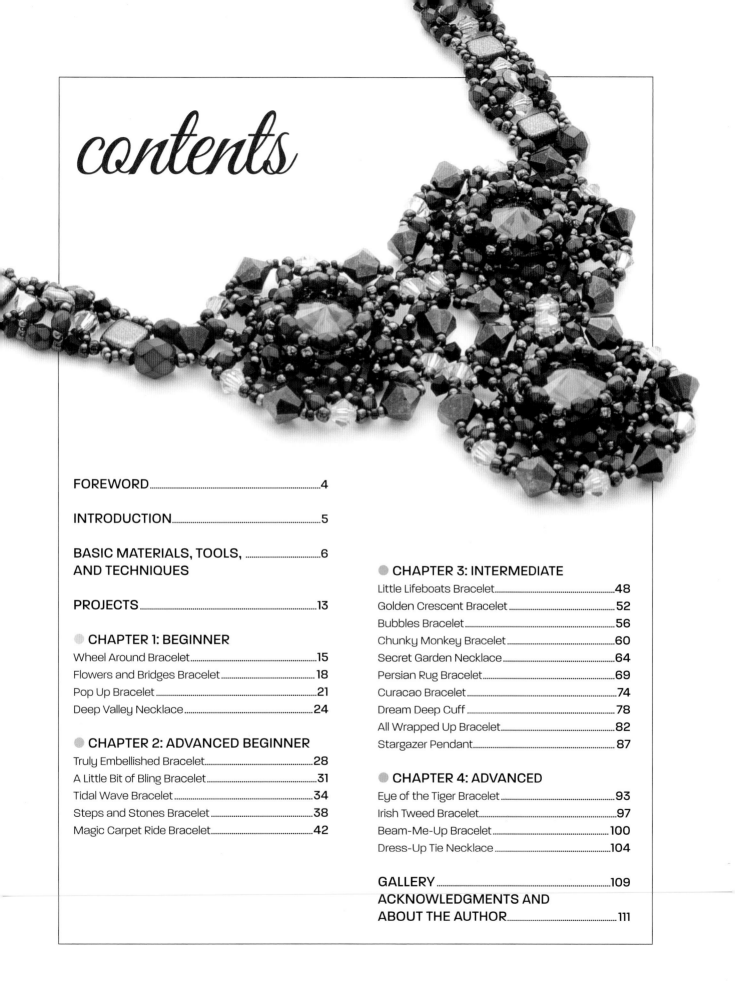

contents

foreword

Though we live on opposite sides of the country, Marcia Balonis and I can attribute our introduction to one little bead and the beading community at my local bead shop, Bead Street in Boise, Idaho. Since my day job includes creating new Czech pressed bead shapes for Starman and I am always eager to listen and learn from fellow beaders, I started taking classes at Bead Street shortly after moving to Boise. Soon after, my pet-project bead, the two-hole Tile, started making its way into stores around the world. As luck would have it, Marcia was one of the first designers to create and distribute her innovative jewelry patterns featuring the two-hole Tile. Plus, Eileen Barker, the owner of Bead Street, and her friend Sandy Taylor were active participants of a nationwide group of bead store owners and teachers who were coordinated by Marcia to test and teach her latest patterns. This arrangement gave me the opportunity to learn Marcia's new techniques as fast as she could create them.

Getting to know Marcia on my own, I was impressed by her eagerness to help further the art of two-hole beading. As I continued to design new two-hole bead shapes, which collectively became known as The CzechMates Two-hole Beading System, the demand for instructional patterns grew. Encouraged by Marcia's enthusiasm, I reached out to more of the emerging two-hole bead advocates, inviting them to join The Starman TrendSetters—a team of designers with the shared goal of creating, teaching, and raising awareness of two-hole beading techniques. As a TrendSetter, Marcia has access to our new bead shapes months before they are released to the public, which has further set her designs ahead of the trends.

Throughout her years as a TrendSetter, it has been my pleasure to witness first-hand how Marcia has become one of the leading bead weaving designers and teachers of our time, for she has continually evolved her stitching methods as the availability of two-hole bead shapes has increased. Her love for beads makes her a natural ambassador for the craft. She excels in all forms of beadwork and is always the first to experiment with new bead shapes, jewelry components, and design concepts. TrendSetter Coordinator, Melinda Barta, attributes much of Marcia's ability to stay on top of trends to her teaching experience: "As an enthusiastic instructor who is very active in the beading community, Marcia's in touch with what students love most and knows how to successfully teach multi-hole bead techniques to beaders of all levels."

I shared Marcia's excitement when she informed me that she was going to write this book. Now is the perfect time for the release of such a comprehensive collection of projects that go beyond the basics and feature her unique style of elegantly embellished, dimensional jewelry designs. Creative thinkers like Marcia are the reason that two-hole beads now have a proven purpose: to transcend the structural limitations of traditional beadwork. This book is not filled with unachievable, one-of-a-kind art pieces; it contains thoughtful, practical jewelry designs that are fun to learn and fashionable to wear.

— Nichole Starman
Director Starman, Inc.
Manufacturer of Czech glass beads, creator of the CzechMates Two-Hole Beading System, founding member of the Starman TrendSetters design team. 2016 Beadwork Magazine Designer of the Year.

introduction

Why beads? What is the pull of those tiny little pieces of glass that captures my hands, mind, and soul? For me, beads are at the core of my life. Beads are the catalyst to satisfy my creative spirit. Beads allow me into a community of like-minded people. They allow me to share my passion and creativity when I teach or communicate with others. They also allow me to escape from the world and exist in the pleasure of a moment in time. The focus of my bead work clears my mind of other flotsam and I stay in that moment without other worries.

For me, beading is a meditative process. One bead at a time to assemble into a little piece of art. I enjoy the creative energy working with my hands and mind to produce something different, something pretty, a statement of hope and joy in the creation.

I love beads. I like to see pretty colors and shapes coming together into a piece reflecting my passion for beading. I am even happier when others like my creations. There is nothing better or more satisfying for me than when a student asks me how I "thought that up." My favorite pieces are those that are created one step at a time with the very last step pulling the piece all together. The last step is often a final connection that works to complete the whole piece and for me it is a magical moment.

Often my beadwork is not a specific stitch. I may use elements of several traditional stitches as building blocks for my construction process. Building blocks with beads, often in layers, to create something unique—and, I hope, happy. I like to bead happy, and I hope you will, too!

— Marcia

basics

TOOLS AND MATERIALS

Needles

Lots of different needles and threads will work. People seem to be very committed to their choice and often get quite passionate about their preference being the correct choice. I do not follow that path. If what you have been using works for you, I don't recommend you change. I'm flexible!

I do have reasons for my preferences. I believe that the Tulip needle is worth the extra price. This needle is stronger, will last longer, and—most important for so many of us—it is easier to thread. This becomes more important as our eyes get older or we get tired. One exception on my needle preference is in the size 13. While the Tulip is great, I actually prefer the longer traditional English beading needle in that size. It won't last as long as the Tulip, but it is less expensive, and I can hold it better to maneuver.

Thread

Thread is a more complex topic. There are so many options and preferences. The five threads I use most often are Fireline 8-lb. test, Nanofil 8- and 10-lb., Power Pro, One G in various colors, and Hana Thread in various colors. The single thread I like the best is Nanofil 10-lb. in green. This fishing line is softer and thinner than Fireline, yet stronger as I use the 10-lb.

The choice of thread or line depends on the beads I plan to use. With crystals or for a heavier piece, I will use Fireline 8-lb. test. If I'm using a lot of crystals, I sometimes switch to Power Pro, which is the strongest thread commonly used by beaders. If you have issues with breakage, I recommend trying Power Pro. The colored threads, One G or Hana, are helpful when thread shows more than usual, such as in a flat peyote piece. Each project in the book will let you know if I have a specific recommendation.

Many beaders use doubled thread in their designs. I seldom use doubled thread, as I prefer to use a heavier weight of line when I feel more thread is needed. There are exceptions where I will use double thread—notably, when building a Dutch spiral piece. None of the projects in this book require double thread; however, if you are used to working that way, go for it!

Conditioner

Conditioners including beeswax or other synthetic products are available to improve thread use. Some people love conditioner to help keep the thread slick. Conditioners also protect the thread a little. I also use it sometimes with threads; it does seem to help.

Thread Zap

My single favorite tool is my Thread Zap. I add thread using the zap to melt the ends of the old and new threads before pulling the knot together. The Thread Zap is available from a variety of different manufacturers. There are YouTube videos showing how to use this tool to add thread as well.

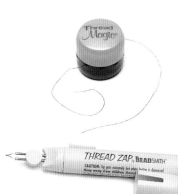

Awl

The Tulip Awl is my next most used tool. The Tulip Awl has a very fine point. It is perfect for popping out a bead. A lot of people smash their beads with a pair of pliers, and I used to do that myself. I would put a needle into the bead hole to protect the thread a little, then smash. I no longer remove a bead that way. I put the awl into the bead and push hard. The bead will snap out. Think of exploding the pieces of glass out and away from the thread versus smashing it in with pliers. There is much less chance of doing damage to your thread by exploding the bead out. The Tulip awl is also great for helping to rip out work or take out a knot.

Bead board

You'll need a bead mat or board of some kind. The "Bead on it Board" is a wonderful invention. Variations exist, and they all are quite similar. I have several of the different brands of boards. For travel, I like the lightweight "Bead on it Board" in the 6x9-in. (15x23cm) size. I use heavier bead boards from other sources when beading on my lap. The difference between boards of this type and a traditional mat is that the beads are easier to pick up. Yes, the advertisement on the bead holes standing up is true! There is also less spillage due to the mat falling off the table or other accidents, which happen more with a loose mat.

Bead scoop

Pick-up tools include scoops, metal triangles, and a razor clam shell-style scoop. The razor clam style is my personal favorite. I have seen people use a baby spoon, which is fun (and probably nostalgic) for the user. And sharp scissors or snips are a must.

Beads

Japanese seed beads

Seed beads are not created equal. As with most things in this world, the quality of the bead varies greatly. This is particularly true of seed beads. Bargain beads will often result in warped beadwork, as the beads are not even. They may also be more apt to lose color. For seed bead work, most patterns are written using one of the two major Japanese seed bead companies: Miyuki or Toho. Both are great bead companies. Even with the precision work of these two companies, you will still need to cull out odd-shaped beads. Consider it another opportunity to stop and admire your work and get into a little Zen focus while beading.

Czech seed beads

Another choice for some projects is seed beads from The Czech Republic. I particularly like traditional Czech beads for bead embroidery. The color of some Czech beads is the best. The Czech Republic has been working with beads, including seed beads, for centuries. Even today recognition of their skill in color and coating is demonstrated by the cooperation of the two major Japanese and Czech companies. Hybrid beads are created in Japan and coated in the Czech Republic. Those are some well-traveled seed beads!

Shaped beads

Shaped beads are not new, and neither are multi-hole beads. I have some vintage beads in my collection from the 1950s that have two holes. I often smile when a new bead comes out, and I look back and find some in my stash from decades ago. A mold may be rediscovered in the Czech Republic, and suddenly you have a "new" bead. Don't get me wrong: Many, many new beads are being newly developed. The Czech Republic is creating and producing pressed beads in a myriad of shapes.

I love both shaped and multi-hole beads. I love the challenge of working with them to see what I can create. My projects are often constructed with a combination of shaped and multi-hole beads. However, I know the market has been flooded with so many new shapes that some are hard to find. Sure, some new shape may be very cool and you want to play with it. I understand as they certainly call to me! But for my book, I wanted to try to use those that are easier to source.

So, I am predominately using shaped beads readily available and produced by Starman. They are the multi-hole beads called CzechMates. These beads are created to work together. The colors and bead holes match. Many projects will also include the popular SuperDuo beads. And yes, for a few projects, I did wander to another shape that worked perfectly in the design.

Crystals

Don't we all love crystals? The shine and bling of a crystal is so attractive, popular, and just plain fun. I use both Swarovski and Preciosa crystals in my work. They come in so many sizes and shapes, and the after-market finishes on some are outstanding. "After-market" refers to a special coating applied by another source after the crystals leave the original manufacturer. I love them all!

Clasps

I love handmade clasps, and I do make them sometimes. I choose clasps that are very easy to use for the wearer. So before I go on, know that clasps are not created equal and what works best for me is not necessarily best for you. In general, I do not use pre-made metal toggles. They are easy to stitch with, but I find they are the most likely to come apart and cause fit problems. Snap clasps, also called ball-and-socket or trailer hitch clasps (just think of the back of big trucks for a visual) are my favorite clasps. They don't take much room, are economical, come in several different colors and finishes, work very easily, are quite secure in designs, and fit easy. For a bigger or more decorative clasp, I use Clasp Garten or Elegant Elements, which are both made by the same company in Germany. I love them. The slide-in bracelet clasp is perfect for a cuff-style bracelet.

TECHNIQUES

Conditioning thread

Use either beeswax (not candle wax or paraffin) or a silicone product to condition nylon thread (Nymo). Beeswax smooths the nylon fibers and adds tackiness that will stiffen your beadwork slightly. Other conditioners add a static charge that causes the thread to repel itself, so don't use it with doubled thread. Stretch the thread, then pull it through the conditioner, starting with the end that comes off the spool first.

Ending and adding thread

To end a thread, weave back into the beadwork, following the existing thread path and tying two or three half-hitch knots around the thread between beads as you go. Change directions as you weave so the thread crosses itself. Sew through a few beads after the last knot before cutting the thread.

To add a thread, start several rows below the point where the last bead was added, and weave through the beadwork, tying half-hitch knots between beads.

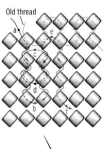

Half-hitch knot

Pass the needle under the thread between two beads. A loop will form as you pull the thread through. Cross over the thread between the beads, sew through the loop, and pull gently to draw the knot into the beadwork.

HELPFUL TERMS

Horizontal construction involves picking up a string of beads for the entire length of the bracelet. Sometimes, this construction style will start with the clasp. Then, the subsequent passes back and forth along the bracelet build out the design. This style really lends itself to using multi-hole beads.

Vertical construction is when the beads are built up one unit at a time with some kind of connection between the units. The connection is often some type of a picot combination. The bracelets made in this style will often have horizontal elements built up on the base later to layer the look.

Picot connections are useful for decorative and construction elements.

Maybe one more connections are useful for decorative and construction elements.

color is key

A common problem for students in local classes is picking color. Many students find this to be a real stumbling block. Students will often want the same exact colors as the designer's sample. Typically, some of those beads will be out of stock or unavailable for various reasons, so color selection becomes an issue.

I often watch customers use several techniques to pick colors. There are some wonderful computer-based options for color selection with different palettes to pick from. I recommend design-seed.com, and there are several others. My issue with this technique is there is no guide for color mixing. How much of one or another color do you use? And on the website, there are SO many to choose from that it makes it hard to pick the one you want to duplicate.

Instead, I prefer to bring a scarf or top to the store that I want to match for a new piece. This is a little better than the computer option because you can also influence the balance of color. The piece will likely have different bead shapes and sizes. When you are trying to match a scarf or top, you can look at the predominant color of the scarf and the beaded piece, and use that to influence your bead choices. It can be a help to balance the color choices to most resemble the look you are trying to achieve.

OTHER IDEAS

I have used other techniques to pick colors. For one bead magazine, I was creating a design for an issue focused on the influence of several artists. I searched the artist's name on a search engine and found several bright, colorful pictures of the artwork. I picked a couple pictures, printed them off, and used the picture as a guide to pick the colors for my samples. When you use art to help you pick your color palette, the artist has done the color mixing for you!

Color is not just about copying another's choice. We all have color preferences and want to create in our favorite colors. Learning to mix colors to please your taste is a skill that comes with practice. Isn't that like life? When selecting seed beads to go along with a primary bead, such as a strand of pearls or fire-polished beads, I will often put two seed beads tubes with the butt end of the tubes touching next to the strand of beads I wish to match. Which of those two colors do I think works the best for my taste? That is what is most important. What do YOU like?

Placing all the beads you want to use next to each other helps. In some patterns, you will even want to place the beads next to each other in the way that they will be used in the bead pattern. Which bead is going to be beside your main bead? Organizing your color palette helps to narrow your choices as well.

This example is for a colorful variation of a simple piece called "Grandma's Button Holes." The seed beads outline the 6mm fire-polished beads. I placed the beads with the butt end of the tubes in line to help decide which colorway I wanted. This is an easy method to help decide which set of beads you want to use when shopping in a store.

Yet another color plan is testing. This is something I still do today in many of my designs. I know before I start a spiral pattern, for example, that it will probably take 3-4 tests of 1 in. (2.5cm) or so before I am happy with the results. I love spiral designs, but to see the way the colors work, it is often best to plan to make up a little sample before finalizing my color choices. Some time spent on testing options is worth every second.

Finally, I often hear from students asking for help "getting out of their box." We do tend to like certain colors more than others. You may gravitate toward the hues you prefer. Before we know it, you have a pile of jewelry in a couple colors or a family of colors and nothing in other colors. Getting out of your box is hard, but worth the rewards. So, I challenge you to step out of the comfortable and try some wild combination. But most of all—bead happy!

projects

beginner

wheel around bracelet

In this fun piece, I used four-hole Lentil beads to create the layers. Just keep track of which hole you're entering as you work around the wheel.

Supplies

- **7–10** 8mm round beads
- **42–60** 3mm round beads (or melons)
- **30–42** 2mm round beads
- **42–60** QuadraLentil beads
- 5g 11º seed beads
- 5g 15º seed beads
- **42–60** prongs
- Two-part clasp
- Scissors
- Beading needle, size 11 or 12
- Fireline, 6-lb. test, or thread of choice

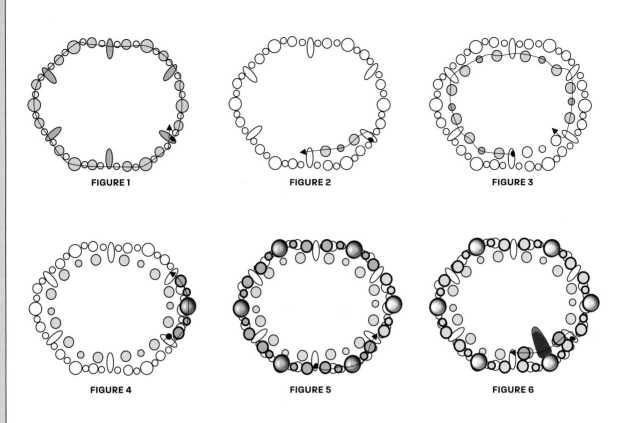

FIGURE 1   **FIGURE 2**   **FIGURE 3**

FIGURE 4   **FIGURE 5**   **FIGURE 6**

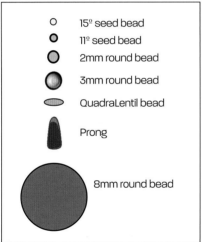

○	15º seed bead
◉	11º seed bead
◯	2mm round bead
⬤	3mm round bead
⬭	QuadraLentil bead
⬮	Prong
⬤	8mm round bead

NOTE: This project uses QuadraLentil beads as the connecting bead between the two rings of beads. QuadraLentils are round lentil beads with four holes like a button. For the first ring, you will sew through the two lower holes (one along the outside edge of the ring and one along the inside edge of the ring). For the second ring, you will use the two upper holes (outside and inside edges of the new ring).

MAKE THE BRACELET

1. Thread a needle on 2 yd. (1.8m) of thread (or the longest piece you are comfortable using).

2. Round 1: The beads in the first round create the lower outside ring. Pick up a QuadraLentil, a 15º seed bead, an 11º seed bead, a 15º, a 2mm round bead, a 15º, an 11º, and a 15º, and repeat five more times to create a ring (you will have six QuadraLentils and six 2mms). Sew through all the beads again to form a ring, leaving a 6-in. (15cm) tail **(figure 1)**. Sew through the beadwork to exit the same hole of the first QuadraLentil.

3. Round 2: Turn to work the lower inside ring by sewing through the adjacent lower hole of the Quadra-Lentil your thread is exiting at the start of this step. Pay attention to which hole you use on this round. Pick up an 11º, a 15º, and an 11º, and sew through the corresponding hole of the next QuadraLentil **(figure 2)**. Repeat to complete the round, and retrace the thread path through all the beads in the round to reinforce **(figure 3)**. Sew through the beads to exit a QuadraLentil.

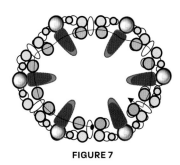

FIGURE 7

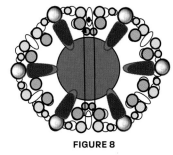

FIGURE 8

FIGURE 9

FIGURE 10

Marcia's Tip

Place your beads in little piles on your beading mat in order of pick up. When you have a lot of beads being used in a specific order, placing the beads this way helps avoid picking up a wrong bead. You'll be able to get into the flow of the beadwork.

4. Round 3: To work the upper outside ring, turn and sew through the upper hole of the next QuadraLentil along the outside edge of the beadwork. Pick up an 11º, a 15º, a 3mm, a 15º, and an 11º, and sew through the corresponding hole of the next QuadraLentil (**figure 4**). The beads in this round will sit on top of the beads in Round 1. Repeat to complete the round (**figure 5**). Retrace the thread path to reinforce the round.

5. Round 4: To complete the ring along the upper inside edge, turn and sew through the upper hole of the next QuadraLentil along the inside edge of the beadwork. Pick up an 11º, a prong, and an 11º, and sew through the corresponding hole of the next Quadra-Lentil (**figure 6**). Repeat around (**figure 7**). Reinforce.

6. Sew through the back inside hole of the next QuadraLentil. Pick up a 15º, an 8mm, and a 15º, and sew into the QuadraLentil directly opposite. Repeat, sewing through the 8mm already picked up (**figure 8**). Retrace the thread path to reinforce, and then sew through the beadwork to exit a 2mm added in round one. You now have one complete unit. The subsequent units are built from the first unit.

7. Round 1 additional units: You will have two shared 2mms between the units. Sew through the beads in round 1 to exit a 2mm to the left of the 8mm connection (highlighted in red). Pick up a 15º, an 11º, a 15º, a QuadraLentil, a 15º, an 11º, a 15º, and a 2mm. Repeat three times. For the next group, pick up a 15º, an 11º, a 15º, a Quadra Lentil, a 15º, a 11º, and a 15º, and sew through the next shared 2mm. Connect from 2mm to 2mm by picking up a 15º, an 11º, a 15º, a QuadraLentil, a 15º, an 11º, and a 15º (**figure 9**). Retrace the thread path to reinforce the round.

8. Create Rounds 2–4 for additional units by repeating steps 3–6, ending and adding thread as needed (Basics, p. 9). The units are all connected from the lower outside ring. Continue adding units to the desired length, minus the clasp. Pay attention and keep the direction of the attachment of the 8mm consistent.

9. For the clasp, exit a 2mm (highlighted red), pick up 1–3 11ºs to fit, and sew through the clasp. Sew back through the beads just added and the beadwork to exit the next 2mm, and repeat (**figure 10**). Retrace the thread path to secure. Repeat on the other end.

flowers and bridges bracelet

A lovely ode to springtime, this piece is worked back and forth along the length of the bracelet. I love the beautiful flowers stitched into this design!

Supplies

- **14–20** 6mm crystal pearls or druk beads
- **44–60** 4mm bicone crystals
- **24–36** 3mm round beads
- **28–36** 2mm true fire-polished beads
- **7–9** SuperDuo beads
- **25–35** 6º seed beads

- 1g 8º seed beads (a pinch)
- 5g 11º seed beads
- 3g 15º seed beads
- Ball-and-socket clasp
- Scissors
- Beading needle, size 10 or 11
- Fireline, 6-lb. test, or thread of choice
- Stop bead

MAKE THE BRACELET

1. Thread a needle on 3 yd. (2.8m) of thread. Attach a stop bead (Basics, p. 9) (highlighted red), leaving a 6-in. (15cm) tail.

2. Row 1: Pick up an 8º seed bead, a 6º seed bead, an 8º, and two 11º seed beads, and repeat to the desired length, ending with an 8º, 6º, and 8º **(figure 1)**. (You must use an odd number of 6ºs. A small bracelet will require 15 6ºs.) Check the sizing at this point. For minor adjustments, you can adjust the size of the clasp or add more beads before the clasp.

3. Row 2: Pick up two 11ºs, an 8º, and one half of the clasp. Working toward the tail, sew back through the 8º just added **(figure 2)**. Pick up two 11ºs, and an 8º, and sew through the 6º. Pick up an 8º, two 11ºs, an 8º, a 6º, an 8º, two 11ºs, and an 8º, skip the next 6º, and sew through the following 6º. Repeat to the end, picking up an 8º, two 11ºs, and an 8º last. Remove the stop bead and pick up the other half of the clasp. Sew back through the final 8º **(figure 3)**. Pull snug.

4. Row 3: Pick up two 11ºs, sew through the next 8º, and continue through the next six beads on this side of the bracelet. Your thread will be exiting a 6º. Pick up an 11º, an 8º, an 11º, a 6mm crystal pearl, an 11º, an 8º, and an 11º, skip the next 6º, and sew through the following 6º **(figure 4)**. Repeat to the second-to-last 6º **(figure 5)**. (Mine requires six 6mms along the side.)

5. Row 4: Sew through the beadwork and repeat step 4 on the opposite side **(figure 6)**.

○	15º seed bead
●	11º seed bead
◯	8º seed bead
◯	6º seed bead
●	2mm fire-polished bead
⬡	3mm round bead
◆	4mm bicone crystal
●	6mm crystal pearl
⬭	SuperDuo bead

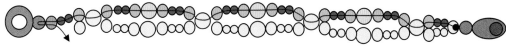

FIGURE 1

FIGURE 2

FIGURE 3

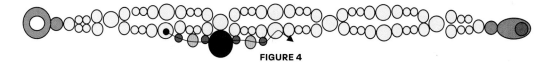

FIGURE 4

FIGURE 5

FIGURE 6

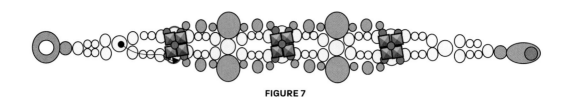

FIGURE 7

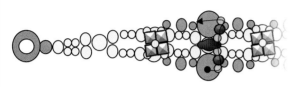

FIGURE 8

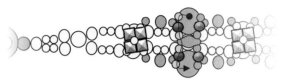

FIGURE 9

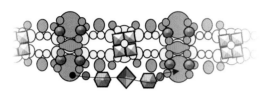

FIGURE 10

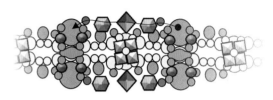

FIGURE 11

PLANT THE FLOWERS

6. Row 5: Sew through the beadwork to exit the second 6º (highlighted red). Pick up a 15º seed bead, a 4mm crystal, a 15º, a crystal, and a 15º, and sew through the corresponding 6º on the other side of the bracelet (highlighted red). (6ºs have different-sized holes. If your 15ºs slip into the 6º's hole, use 11ºs instead.) You are crossing over the bracelet on the diagonal. Pick up a 15º and a crystal, and sew through the second 15º picked up at the start of this step. Pick up a crystal and a 15º, and sew through the first 6º in this step to finish your flower (**figure 7**). Repeat to the end, referring to figure 7 for placement.

hint **If you can see the difference in the shape of the crystal (that one side is more pointed than the other), place the narrower point in the center. It will result in a better flower.**

MAKE THE BRIDGES

7. Row 6: Sew through the beadwork to exit the next 6mm. Pick up a 15º, a 2mm fire-polished bead, a 15º, a SuperDuo bead, a 15º, a 2mm, and a 15º, and sew through the 6mm on the other side of the bracelet (**figure 8**). Pick up a 15º, a 2mm, and a 15º, and sew through the adjacent hole of the SuperDuo. Pick up a 15º, a 2mm, and a 15º, and sew through the original 6mm (**figure 9**). Repeat to build bridges between all of the 6mms along the bracelet.

MAKE THE WINGS

8. Row 7: Sew through the beadwork to exit a 6mm. Pick up an 11º, a 3mm round bead, a crystal, a 3mm, and an 11º, and sew through the next 6mm. Repeat to add wings between all the 6mms along the bracelet (**figure 10**).

9. Row 8: Sew through the beadwork and repeat step 8 on the opposite side (**figure 11**). Reinforce the sides and end the thread.

Marcia's Tip

Stretch your thread! This is particularly important with beading threads such as One G, C-Lon, Hana, or similar. Stretching will help to remove any memory of the smaller bobbin, remove kinks, and prevent the finished work from stretching and gaping later.

pop up
bracelet

The piece layers from a right-angle weave base. The base is completed with two needles. The buildup is a series of picots followed by a bridge connection.

Supplies

- **16–20** 6mm top-drilled round beads
- **60–72** 4mm glass rondelle beads
- **30–48** 4mm round or fire-polished beads
- **41–50** 3mm fire-polished, melon, or English-cut beads
- **24–30** 2mm round beads
- 10g 11º seed beads
- 5g 15º seed beads (in **2** colors, if desired)
- Ball-and-socket clasp
- Scissors
- Beading needle, size 10 or 11
- Fireline, 6-lb. test, or thread of choice

MAKE THE BRACELET

1. Thread a needle on each end of about 3 yd. (2.7m) of thread, leaving about 4–6 in. (10–15cm) of tail on each end. This piece will start at the midpoint of the thread. You will work the base for the right-angle weave boxes with two needles.

2. On one needle, pick up a 6mm top-drilled bead, a 4mm rondelle bead, a 4mm round bead, a rondelle, and a 6mm. With the other needle, pick up a rondelle, a 4mm round, and a rondelle, and sew through the 6mm picked up on the other needle in the opposite direction so the thread is exiting each side of the 6mm **(figure 1)**.

FIGURE 1

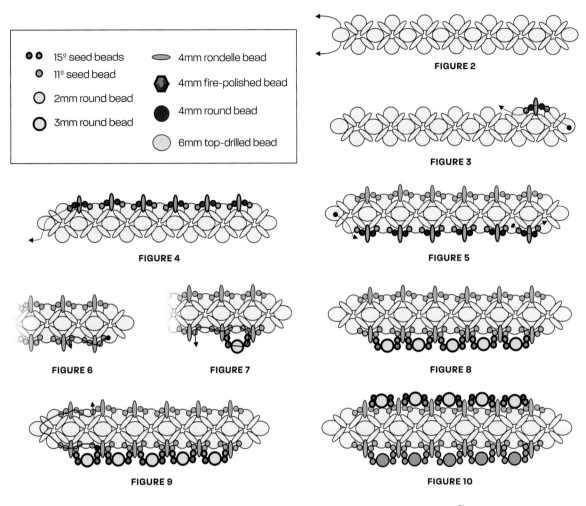

Legend:
- ●● 15º seed beads
- ● 11º seed bead
- ◯ 2mm round bead
- ◎ 3mm round bead
- ⬭ 4mm rondelle bead
- ⬡ 4mm fire-polished bead
- ● 4mm round bead
- ◯ 6mm top-drilled bead

FIGURE 2

FIGURE 3

FIGURE 4

FIGURE 5

FIGURE 6

FIGURE 7

FIGURE 8

FIGURE 9

FIGURE 10

3. Continue to pick up a rondelle, a 4mm round, a rondelle, and a 6mm with one needle, and a rondelle, a 4mm round, and a rondelle with the other needle, and sew through the 6mm. You will always have a needle exiting both sides of the 6mm. Continue in this pattern for the length of the bracelet **(figure 2)**. (Leave room for the clasp.)

4. Next, you will work the first layer of picot edge along the sides. This is done one needle at a time, so just park a needle in your bead mat. With the remaining needle, sew through the beadwork to exit an edge 4mm round. Pick up a 15º seed bead, an 11º seed bead, a rondelle, an 11º, and a 15º, and sew through the next 4mm round **(figure 3)**. Repeat along this side for the length of the bracelet, and then sew through the beadwork to exit the edge 6mm **(figure 4)**.

5. Sew through the beadwork to exit the first 4mm round on the next side, and fill in as in step 5 **(figure 5)**. You might even like how it looks now with the little picot sticking out! Notice how the rondelle sits in between the two rondelles of the first row to form a "Y" shape. Do not end the thread.

6. Remove the other needle from the bead mat, and sew through the beadwork to exit the 11º next to the rondelle in the picot, pointing away from the bracelet (highlighted red) **(figure 6)**.

7. Add the second layer of picot beads: Pick up two 15ºs, a 3mm round, and two 15ºs (I used different colors for my 15ºs), and sew back through the 11º. Sew through the beadwork along the picot edge to the next 11º after the next 4mm fire-polished bead (the two 11ºs used are shown red) **(figure 7)**. Repeat all along the side of the bracelet **(figure 8)**.

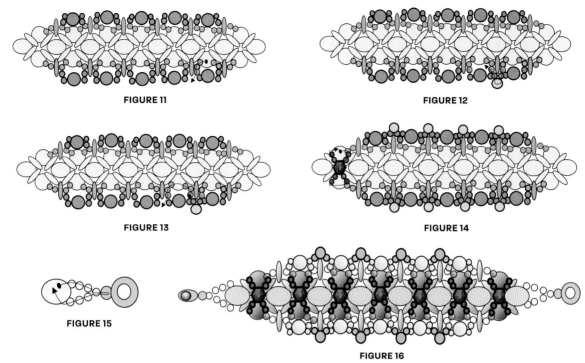

FIGURE 11

FIGURE 12

FIGURE 13

FIGURE 14

FIGURE 15

FIGURE 16

8. Sew through the beadwork to exit the 11º beyond the first picot rondelle **(figure 9)**. Repeat step 8 to add a second picot on this side **(figure 10)**.

9. To add the third picot layer, sew through the base beadwork to exit the 15º next to the first 3mm round (highlighted red) **(figure 11)**. Pick up an 11º, a 2mm round, and an 11º, and sew through the next base 15º (highlighted red) **(figure 12)**. This picot hugs the rondelle. Sew through the beadwork to exit the next base 15º (highlighted red) **(figure 13)**, and repeat this step. Repeat along both sides.

10. The final step creates little bridges over the gap between the 4mm rounds: Exit an end 4mm round. Pick up a 15º, an 11º, a 3mm round, an 11º, and a 15º, and sew through the opposite 4mm round on the diagonal. Pick up an 11º and a 15º, and sew through the 3mm. Pick up a 15º and an 11º, and sew through the first 4mm round **(figure 14)**. Repeat this step on the remaining pairs of 4mm rounds for the length of the bracelet.

11. At the end of the bracelet, exit a 6mm. Pick up four 11ºs and half of the clasp, and sew back through the last 11º picked up. Pick up three 11ºs, and sew through the 6mm from the opposite direction **(figure 15)**. Retrace the thread path through the clasp connection to secure **(figure 16)**. Repeat on the other end of the bracelet, and end the threads.

Marcia's Tip

The secret to taking out knots is two needles. When you get a knot, it will come out more easily if you first poke one needle into the knot, then poke at the knot with another needle. This way, you are opening the knot up from the stable needle in the knot.

Of course, the goal is to learn to catch knots before they form. To avoid knots: As you pull your thread through your beads, watch the working thread to see if it is spinning around itself. That is often the first step to a knot, and you'll want to separate the threads to avoid it.

If you already have a little knot developing, it is best to take it out right away and not hope that it will "pull out." And don't take too much thread! Adding thread isn't that hard. You will spend more time taking out knots than adding thread if you take a longer piece than is comfortable for you to use without knotting.

deep valley necklace

The DNA spiral is one of the easiest and most versatile stitches. If you are a beginner, this necklace is the perfect way to learn basic spiral. By the time you finish the base, you will be ready to take it to the next level with the embellishment.

Supplies

- **150** 4mm round or fire-polished beads
- **300** 2mm or 3mm bicone crystals or fire-polished beads
- **300** O-beads
- 15g 6º seed beads
- 10g 8º seed beads
- 11º seed beads in **2** colors: 10g color A and 7g color B
- 5g 15º seed beads
- Scissors
- Beading needle, size 10 or 11
- Fireline, 6-lb. test, or thread of choice
- Clasp

 To create the look of the valley, you need to select your colors accordingly. Core beads and loop seed beads should be dramatically different from the O-beads and 4mm round beads in the loop and embellishment. The illustrations show a contrast using blue for the center of the loop and embellishment.

MAKE THE NECKLACE

1. You will need 12–15 yd. (11–13.7m) of thread for a necklace 20 in. (51cm) long without the clasp, so plan to add thread as you work. Thread a needle on the longest thread you are comfortable using (I usually take about a wing span plus a little).

2. Pick up four 6º seed beads (core) and a color A 11º seed bead, a color B 11º seed bead, an 8º seed bead, an O-bead, a 4mm round, an O-bead, an 8º, a B, and an A (**figure 1**), leaving an 8-in. (20cm) tail. This is a nine-bead loop pattern.

3. Sew through the four 6º core beads again in the same direction to form a loop of beads (**figure 2**). This finishes the start-up pattern.

4. For the repeating loop pattern: Pick up a 6º (core) an A, a B, an 8º, an O-bead, a 4mm, an O-bead, an 8º, a B, and an A. Snug up the beads, and sew through the last three core beads added in the previous step (highlighted white) and the one core bead added in this step (**figure 3**). Do not sew through the very first core bead on the thread. You will be adding one new core bead with each loop. Each loop will lay on top of the previous loop.

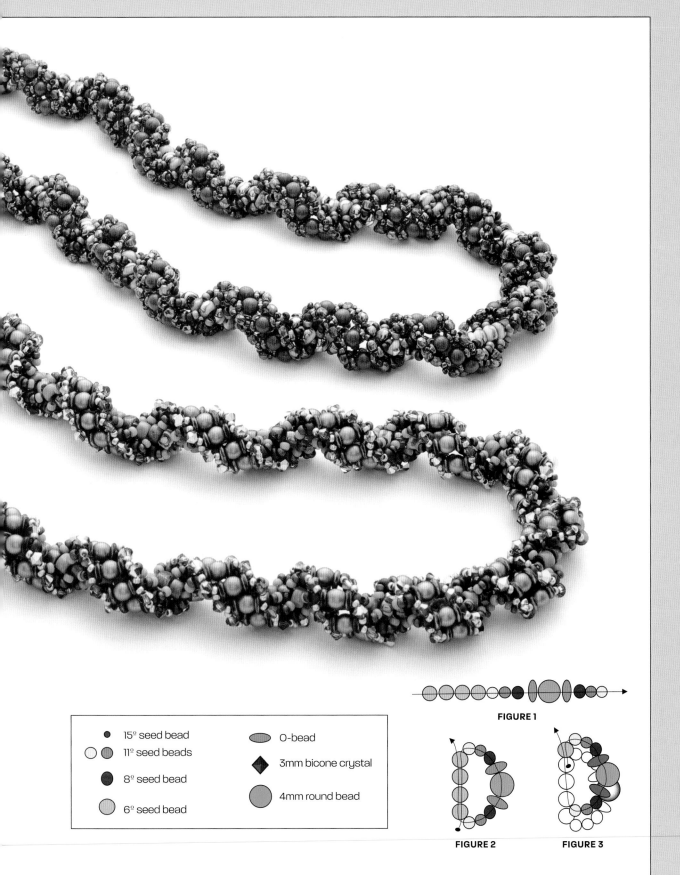

FIGURE 1

FIGURE 2

FIGURE 3

- ● 15º seed bead
- ○ ● 11º seed beads
- ● 8º seed bead
- ● 6º seed bead
- ⬭ O-bead
- ◆ 3mm bicone crystal
- ● 4mm round bead

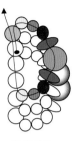

FIGURE 4

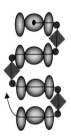

FIGURE 5

FIGURE 6

FIGURE 7

5. Continue to pick up one core bead and the nine-bead loop pattern to the desired finished length, ending and adding thread as needed. Pull the thread tight, and push the nine-loop beads over so they sit next to the previous loop **(figure 4)**. You can work from either the left or right when pushing the beads over to spiral, but you must be consistent. This piece will shrink a little after the embellishment is added, so make the beadwork a tad longer than your desired length (about ¼–½ in./6–13mm).

6. The embellishment is stitched in a wave pattern from end to end to connect the 4mms with other bead(s). Sew through the beadwork to exit an O-bead after a 4mm at one end of the rope. Pick up a combination of bead(s) of your choice, and sew through the O-bead, 4mm, and O-bead **(figure 5)**. Repeat to the end, adding the connection in a wave. At the end, turn and head back the other way to fill in the other side of the three accent beads so each set of three accent beads is encased in your choice of embellishment beads **(figure 6)**. The embellishment combination could be a 3mm crystal, or some seed bead combination; play with what fits with your accent beads. I used a pattern of a 15º seed bead, a 3mm bicone crystal, and a 15º.

7. To attach the clasp, sew through the beadwork to exit an end core bead. Pick up an 11º, a 15º (if desired) and one half of the clasp, and sew back through the 15º and 11º, and continue through the first few core beads **(figure 7)**. Then sew through the beadwork to retrace the thread path through the clasp again several times to secure. Repeat on the other end, and end the threads.

Marcia's Tip

Gravity is your friend! To avoid tangles and sew cleanly, hold your beadwork upside down so you are sewing into the piece. This will cause fewer tangles or catches.

First, put your needle and thread through the bead or beads you need to pass through for that step. Then, as you start to pull your thread through the work, lift up enough for the working thread to be below your work.

When you use this technique, gravity will weigh the beads being added down below your beadwork. As you pull your needle and thread through the beadwork, watch your thread and at the end of it, you can turn back over. That way, there is nothing for the thread to snag on. This is particularly helpful when you have a lot of protruding beads or bigger beads in your weaving.

advanced
beginner

truly embellished bracelet

This is a great beginner piece for adding odd-count peyote to your weaving skills. This lesson assumes you already know basic, even-count peyote. Odd-count peyote is a little harder, but for any centered design of color or embellishment, it is necessary. This project can vary in width based on the number of beads you use at the start. But stick with an odd number!

Supplies

- **80** 2mm fire-polished beads
- 15–20g 8º seed beads
- 10g 11º seed beads
- 2g 15º seed beads
- four- or five-loop strand bar slide clasp
- Scissors
- Beading needle, size 10
- Fireline, 6-lb. test, or thread of choice
- Bead stopper

◉	15º seed bead
○	11º seed bead
◯	8º seed bead
⬡	2mm fire-polished bead

MAKE THE BRACELET

1. Thread a needle on the longest piece of thread you are comfortable using. I needed over 4 yd. (3.7m) in total for my bracelet, but you may not want to work with that much at one time (and it is very easy to add thread in peyote stitch). Attach a bead stopper on the end of the thread, leaving an 8-in. (20cm) tail, and pick up 13 8º seed beads (or any odd number) for the desired width **(figure 1)**. These beads will form the first two rows once the third row is added.

2. Row 3: Pick up an 8º, skip an 8º, and sew through the next 8º. Repeat this stitch to the end of the row. You will use seven beads (or another odd number) **(figure 2)**. Every other row in odd-count peyote stitch changes. At the end of the row, tie the working thread and tail together, and then turn and sew through the last bead added so the needle is pointing in the opposite direction **(figure 3)**. (You will only tie the thread here, at the beginning. The turn for subsequent rows will change.)

3. Row 4: Pick up an 8º, skip an 8º, and sew through the next 8º. Repeat to the end of the row. This row adds an even number of beads and does not require a special turn **(figure 4)**.

4. Row 5: Pick up an 8º, skip an 8º, and sew through the next seed bead. Repeat to the end of the row **(figure 5)**. This row adds an odd number of beads and therefore requires an odd-count turn at the end of the row. I use the "catch a thread" method, but there are other techniques. To turn, sew under the thread from the previous two side beads, and sew back through the last 8º added **(figure 6)**. This is similar to the thread catch used in brick stitch. Repeat steps 3 and 4 to the desired length, ending and adding thread as needed.

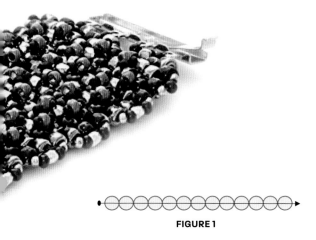

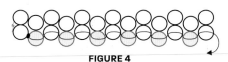

FIGURE 1

FIGURE 2

FIGURE 3

FIGURE 4

FIGURE 5

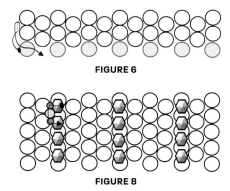

FIGURE 6

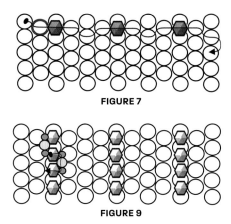

FIGURE 7

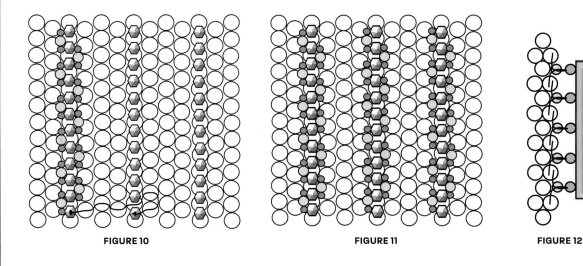

FIGURE 8

FIGURE 9

5. Embellishment is fun and can be done so many ways. For this piece, I used a "fill the ditch" method using fire-polished beads for the first layer followed with a zig-zag connection using seed beads. To fill the ditch using 2mm fire-polished beads, sew through the beadwork to exit the second bead in from the side (highlighted red) **(figure 7)**. Pick up a 2mm, skip over the gap, and sew through the next bead. Sew through two beads to get into position for the next row. The first row of filling the ditch and your travel path is shown in **figure 7**. You are working the width of the bracelet. At the end of each row, turn, using the edge beads to the next row to fill the ditch in line with the first row.

6. After completing the "fill the ditch" technique, sew through the beadwork to exit the first 2mm at either end. You will add beads along the column of 2mms. Pick up a 15º seed bead, an 11º seed bead, and a 15º, and sew on through the next 2mm in the column **(figures 8 and 9)**. Repeat for the length of the bracelet, and then sew through the beadwork to exit the end 2mm in the

next column (watch your approach if you want to embellish the same way) **(figure 10)**. Continue to embellish all the 2mm columns **(figure 11)**.

7. Make a side picot with a pleasing combination of seed beads and 2mms. I made mine by exiting an end 8º along one edge. Pick up a 15º, an 11º, a 2mm, an 11º, and a 15º, skip the next edge 8º, and sew down through the following 8º and up through the next edge 8º. Repeat for the length of the bracelet, and then sew through the beadwork to exit an end 8º along the opposite edge. Repeat to embellish the other edge.

8. To attach the clasp, sew through the beadwork to exit an end 8º with the needle pointing toward the opposite edge. Pick up a 15º and a loop of one half of the clasp, and sew back through the 15º. Continue through the end 8º **(figure 12)**. Repeat until you have attached all the loops, and then retrace the thread path to reinforce. Repeat on the other end of the bracelet, and end the threads.

FIGURE 10

FIGURE 11

FIGURE 12

a little bit of bling bracelet

There are lots of possibilities for alternatives if you select different beads. Use my version as an example, but feel free to explore the unique design potential of many different types of beads.

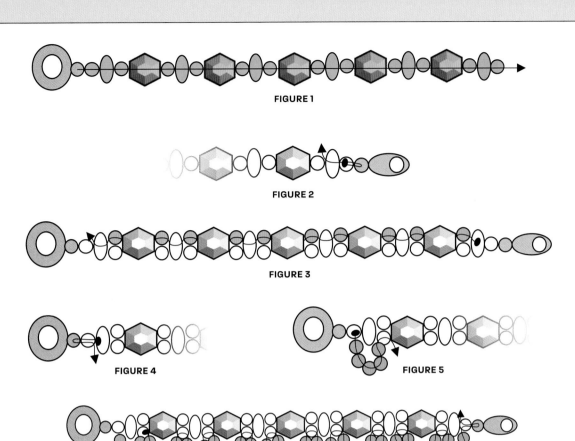

FIGURE 1

FIGURE 2

FIGURE 3

FIGURE 4

FIGURE 5

FIGURE 6

Supplies

- **12–17** 6mm round or fire-polished beads
- **48–68** 4mm bicone crystals
- **13–18** 3x4mm or 4x6mm rondelle beads
- **22–28** 3.4mm drop beads
- 10g 11º seed beads
- Ball-and-socket clasp
- Scissors
- Beading needle, size 10 or 11
- Fireline, 6-lb. test, or thread of your choice

MAKE THE BRACELET

1. Cut 3 yd. (2.7m) of Fireline, and thread a needle on one end. Tie one half of the clasp to the center of the thread (see "Marcia's Tip," p. 46). Pick up an 11º seed bead, a 3x4mm rondelle bead, an 11º, and a 6mm fire-polished bead. Repeat to the desired length, ending with a rondelle followed by an 11º **(figure 1)**.

2. Pick up the other half of the clasp, and sew back through the 11º and rondelle **(figure 2)**.

3. Pick up an 11º, and sew through the next 6mm. Pick up an 11º, and sew through the next rondelle. Repeat for the entire length of the bracelet. There will be two side-by-side 11ºs **(figure 3)**. Sew through the loop of the clasp again to reinforce, and exit the first 11º **(figure 4)**.

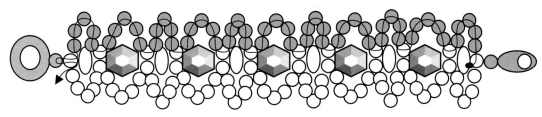

FIGURE 7

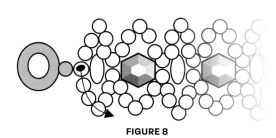

FIGURE 8

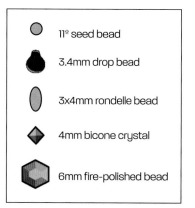

11º seed bead

3.4mm drop bead

3x4mm rondelle bead

4mm bicone crystal

6mm fire-polished bead

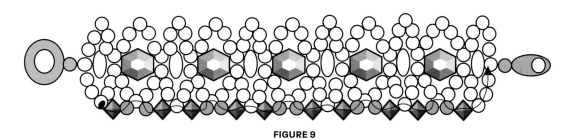

FIGURE 9

4. Pick up five 11ºs, and sew through the next 11º to make a picot **(figure 5)**. Repeat for the length of the band, being careful not to twist the bracelet; stay on one side of the pair of 11ºs. Sew through the loop of the clasp to reinforce, and sew back through the end 11º **(figure 6)**.

hint **If you think you will have a hard time finding the middle bead of the five beads, use two colors: Pick up two of color A, one of color B, and two more of color A.**

5. Repeat step 4 to make the picots on the other side of the band **(figure 7)**. Reinforce the clasp as before.

6. Use the other half of the thread from step 1 to continue. Sew through the beadwork to exit the center 11º in the five-bead picot **(figure 8)**. Pick up a 4mm bicone crystal and an 11º, and sew through the center 11º in the next picot. Pick up an 11º and a crystal, and sew through the next center 11º **(figure 9)**. Repeat to the end of the bracelet. Be sure to avoid twisting the band as you connect the beads.

7. Work as in step 6 to embellish the other side of the bracelet. End the threads.

tidal wave bracelet

This is a fun piece to work! I used the traditional box-style right-angle weave (RAW), which I expanded to incorporate SuperDuos and O-beads.

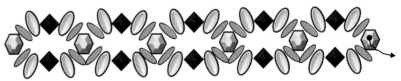

Supplies

- **30** 4mm fire-polished beads
- **30** 4mm bicone crystals
- **30** 3mm fire-polished beads
- **132** 2mm fire-polished beads
- 5g O-beads
- 5g SuperDuo beads
- 5g 15º seed beads
- Toggle clasp
- Scissors
- Beading needle, size 10 or 11
- Fireline, 6-lb. test, or thread of choice

FIGURE 1

FIGURE 2

MAKE THE BRACELET

1. Thread a needle on a comfortable length of Fireline. You'll create a RAW base with one needle (if you want to use a two-needle technique, go for it!). Pick up 4mm fire-polished bead, an O-bead, a SuperDuo bead, a 4mm bicone crystal, a SuperDuo, an O-bead, a 4mm fire-polished bead, an O-bead, a SuperDuo, a crystal, a SuperDuo, and an O-bead, leaving a 6-in. (15cm) tail. You now have the first set of 12 beads, which forms the base (**figure 1**). Sew through all the beads again to form a ring, and continue through the first seven beads to exit the 4mm fire-polished bead opposite the tail.

2. The repeating pattern for the base of the bracelet uses the center 4mm fire-polished bead as the shared bead: Pick up an O-bead, a SuperDuo, a crystal, a SuperDuo, an O-bead, a 4mm fire-polished bead, an O-bead, a SuperDuo, a crystal, a SuperDuo, and an O-bead (**figure 2**). Sew through the first 4mm fire-polished bead your thread exited at the start of this step, and continue through the next six beads to exit the end 4mm fire-polished bead. Repeat this step for the

desired length, leaving room for the clasp. This piece will shrink a little.

3. Once you reach the desired length, I recommend you fully reinforce the last unit to secure, and exit the O-bead after the 4mm fire-polished bead, pick up two 15° seed beads, and sew through the available hole of the SuperDuo hole (**figure 3**).

4. Next, you will work the first row down both sides. Pick up a 15° a 2mm fire-polished bead, a 15°, a 2mm, and a 15°, and sew through the available hole of the next SuperDuo (**figure 4**).

5. Pick up a SuperDuo, and sew through the available hole of the next SuperDuo (**figure 5**). Repeat steps 4 and 5 to the end of this side of the bracelet. Pick up two 15°s, and sew through the next three beads to exit the end O-bead along the opposite edge. You will notice the added SuperDuo is protruding. Sew through the beadwork from the edge to edge SuperDuos using two 15°s as in step 3 in both corners (**figure 6**).

FIGURE 3

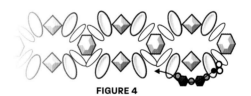

FIGURE 4

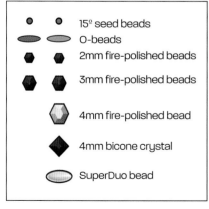

● ●	15° seed beads
⬬ ⬬	O-beads
⬢ ⬢	2mm fire-polished beads
⬢ ⬢	3mm fire-polished beads
⬢	4mm fire-polished bead
◆	4mm bicone crystal
⬭	SuperDuo bead

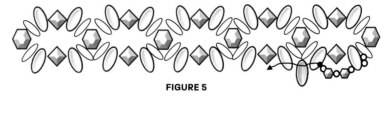

FIGURE 5

FIGURE 6

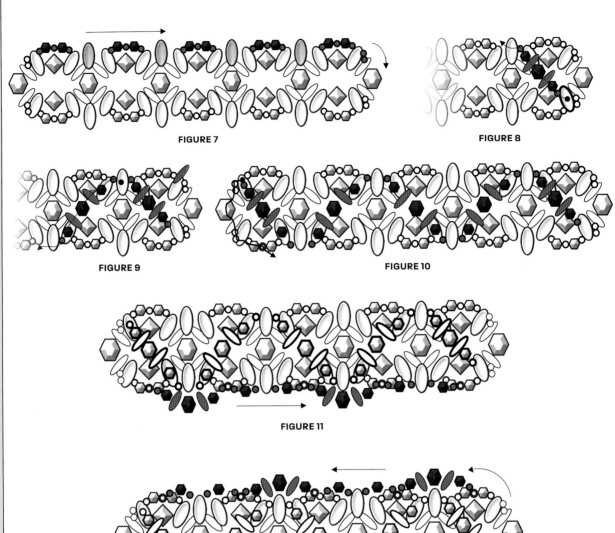

FIGURE 7

FIGURE 8

FIGURE 9

FIGURE 10

FIGURE 11

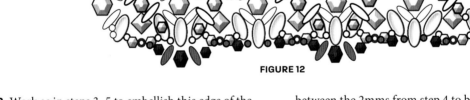

FIGURE 12

6. Work as in steps 3–5 to embellish this edge of the base, ending and adding thread as needed **(figure 7)**. Don't forget the two 15ºs at the corners!

7. To create the wave pattern down the center: Exit the same hole of the first SuperDuo added in step 5. Pick up a 15º a 2mm, an O-bead, a 3mm fire-polished bead, an O-bead, a 2mm, and a 15º, and, crossing the base on the diagonal, sew through the corresponding hole of the next SuperDuo on the other side **(figure 8)**. Repeat this stitch to create a wave pattern along the bracelet **(figure 9)**. Sew through the beadwork to exit the center 15º

between the 2mms from step 4 to be in position to start the next row **(figure 10)**.

8. As you embellish the sides of the bracelet, note that your pattern may be slightly different, depending on the length of your base. Pick up a 15º, a 2mm, and O-bead, a 3mm, an O-bead, a 2mm, and a 15º. Skip the next SuperDuo added in step 5, and sew through the center 15º in the picot from step 6 (highlighted red in **figure 11**). Pick up a 15º, a 2mm, and a 15º, and sew through the available hole of the next SuperDuo. Pick up a 15º, a 2mm, and a 15º, and sew through the center 15º in the

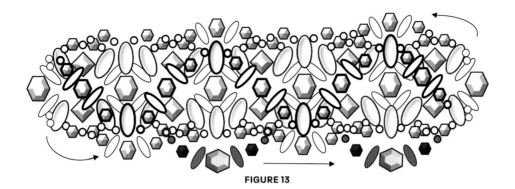

FIGURE 13

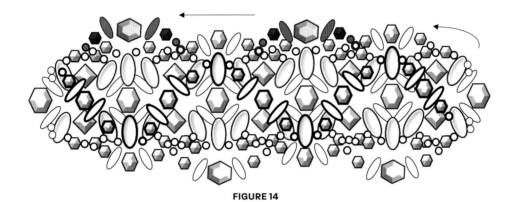

FIGURE 14

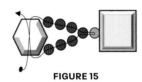

FIGURE 15

next picot. Sew through the beadwork to exit the center 15º between the 2mms from step 4 along the opposite edge. Repeat this step (note that in the repeat, the bead pickup will be in the opposite order) **(figure 12)**.

9. Sew through the beadwork around the end of the bracelet, retracing the longer picot from step 8, to reach the other side. Exit the 15º following either the first 2mm after the SuperDuo, or the first 2mm after the first picot with the O-bead and 3mm (highlighted red). You are simply filling what should be a big gap. Adjust your bead count slightly, if needed. This should poke up the SuperDuo to give dimension. Pick up a 15º, a 2mm, an O-bead, a 4mm fire-polished bead, an O-bead, a 2mm, and a 15º **(figure 13)**. Sew through the 15º, following the picot from step 8, but before the 2mm, and sew through the beadwork to repeat. Repeat this step along the other side of the band **(figure 14)**.

10. To attach the clasp, sew through the beadwork to exit an end 4mm fire-polished bead. Pick up four 11º seed beads and one half of the clasp, and sew back through the last 11º. Pick up three 11ºs, and sew through the end bead in the same direction **(figure 15)**. Retrace the thread path a few times to secure, and end the working thread. Thread a needle on the tail, and repeat.

Marcia's Tip

If you think you will have a hard time finding the middle bead of the five beads, use two colors: Pick up two of color A, one of color B, and two more of color A.

steps and stones bracelet

This is a basic flat herringbone stitch, which I've embellished with lots of sparkling goodies. Pay careful attention to the illustrations to follow thread path.

Supplies

- **24–34** CzechMate Tile beads
- **72–106** 3mm bicone crystals
- **12–17** SuperDuo beads
- 15g 8º seed beads
- 5g 11º seed beads
- 5g 15º seed beads
- Multi-strand clasp
- Scissors
- Beading needle, size 11
- Fireline, 6-lb. test, or thread of your choice

	15º seed bead
	11º seed bead
	8º seed bead
◆	3mm bicone crystal
	SuperDuo bead
	Tile bead

FIGURE 1

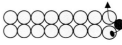

FIGURE 2

FIGURE 3

FIGURE 4

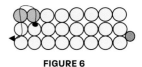

FIGURE 5

FIGURE 6

FIGURE 7

Marcia's Tip

Many times, you can start with a clasp or add the clasp during the process. When you do that, you are taking a chance that if the clasp breaks or you want to change it for some other reason, your work will be compromised. When you use a new thread or well-secured working thread, you can be confident that if you cut off the clasp, your work is still solid. If you prefer not to start with a clasp, you can always use a soldered jump ring and attach a clasp later.

MAKE THE BRACELET

1. This flat base starts with an eight-bead wide and two-bead high ladder stitch. Thread a needle on a comfortable length of beading thread, and pick up four 8º seed beads, sew back through all the beads again, leaving a 6-in. (15cm) tail. Adjust the beads into two columns or a box **(figure 1)**. To increase the length of the ladder, you will add two beads to the side—not the top. Pick up two 8ºs, and sew through the last two 8ºs you just exited, and continue through the two 8ºs you just added **(figures 2 and 3)**. Repeat until you reach the desired width (minus the clasp). My bracelet is eight beads wide. To make the turn at the end of the row and be in position for the next row, pick up an 11º seed bead and sew up through the second-to-last 8º added **(figure 4)**.

2. Herringbone stitch is completed with two beads at a time in columns. Pick up two 8ºs, and sew back down through the next 8º in the two-bead column **(figure 5)**. Sew up through the next 8º. Repeat this stitch across the row **(figure 6)**. At the edge, turn using an 11º or 15º seed bead **(figure 7)**.

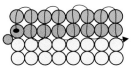

FIGURE 8

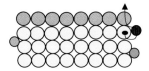

FIGURE 9

1 2 3 4 5 6 7 8

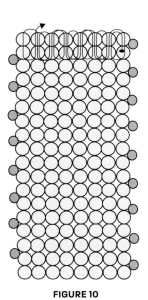

FIGURE 10

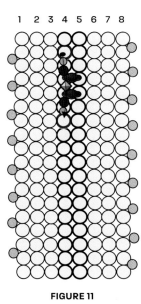

FIGURE 11

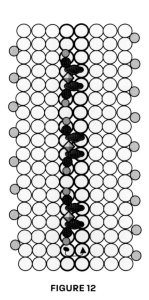

FIGURE 12

advanced beginner

3. Continue to work in herringbone stitch across the row, two beads at a time **(figure 8)**. At the edge, turn with an 11º **(figure 9)**. (These 11º turn beads do not perfectly align.) Work to reach the desired length, minus the clasp, ending and adding thread as needed. Make sure the number of rows is divisible by 5 plus 3. For a 6-in. (15cm) bracelet without clasp, you'll need 63 rows. For a 7-in. (18cm) bracelet, you'll need 73 rows.

4. Follow a ladder stitch thread path through the beads in the last two rows to end the bracelet length **(figure 10)**.

CENTER EMBELLISHMENT
5. To embellish the band, sew through the beadwork to exit an 8º in the four column, second row from the end (highlighted red). Pick up a 15º, an 11º, a SuperDuo bead, a 3mm crystal, a SuperDuo, an 11º, and a 15º. Skip four 8ºs in the same column, and sew through the fifth 8º in the base (also highlighted red) **(figure 11)**. Repeat to the end of the band. Turn and sew through the adjacent 8º in the other middle row, with the needle pointing toward the opposite end of the band **(figure**

12). Repeat this step, but instead of adding a new SuperDuo, sew through the available hole of the SuperDuo added in the previous column **(figure 13)**.

6. The Tile beads are added on either side of the center embellishment. Exit the corresponding 8º in the next column. Pick up a 15º, an 11º, a Tile, an 11º, and a 15º **(figure 14)**. Skip four 8ºs, and sew through the fifth 8º. Repeat to the end of the band. Turn by sewing through the corresponding 8º in the adjacent row **(figure 15)**. Repeat this step, but instead of picking up a Tile, sew through the available hole of the Tile added in the previous column. Sew through the beadwork to exit the 8º second from the end in the third column. Repeat this step to add the Tile embellishment on this side of the bracelet **(figure 16)**.

7. Sew through the beadwork to fill in along the edge between the 11º turn beads. Pick up a crystal and a 15º, and sew through the next 11º along the edge. Repeat to the end of the bracelet **(figure 17)**, and then repeat along the remaining edge. Note there is a wave to

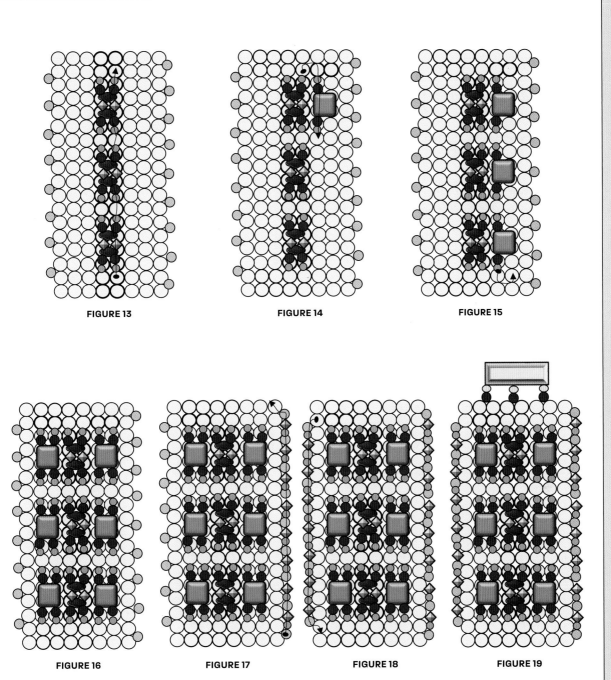

FIGURE 13   FIGURE 14   FIGURE 15

FIGURE 16   FIGURE 17   FIGURE 18   FIGURE 19

herringbone, and the order of these two beads will fit better in one direction than the other. In **figure 18**, the beads were picked up in the opposite order.

8. Add a clasp with one or two 11ºs centered over two edge beads: Pick up one or two 11ºs, and pass through a hole of the clasp. Pass back through the the 11º closest to the clasp, and sew through the beadwork to exit the next pair of 8ºs. Repeat to attach the remaining holes of the clasp (**figure 19**). Reinforce the thread path. Repeat on the other side of the bracelet to attach the other half of the clasp.

magic carpet ride bracelet

This bracelet consists of a base layer and a Crescent bead embellishment layer that sits on top of the base layer and is connected through the top holes of the QuadraTile beads.

Supplies
- **48–64** Crescent beads
- **48–64** QuadraTile beads
- 18g SuperDuo beads
- 10g 8º seed beads
- 11º seed beads in **2** colors: 5g color A, 1g color B
- 5g 15º seed beads in **2** colors (if desired)
- Three-strand clasp
- Scissors
- Beading needle, size 11 or 12
- Fireline, 6-lb. test, or thread of your choice
- Stop bead
- Spool (optional)

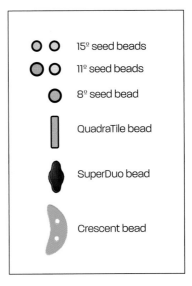

○ ○	15º seed beads
◉ ○	11º seed beads
◉	8º seed bead
▌	QuadraTile bead
◆	SuperDuo bead
◗	Crescent bead

FIGURE 1

MAKE THE BRACELET

1. Thread a needle on the longest thread you are comfortable using (see "Marcia's Tip," p. 46).

2. Attach a stop bead (Basics, p. 9), leaving a 12–15-in. (30–38cm) tail. Pick up a SuperDuo bead and three 15º seed beads, and sew through the available hole of the same SuperDuo **(figure 1)**. Pick up two Super-Duos, a color A 11º seed bead, an 8º seed bead, an A, a QuadraTile bead, an A, an 8º, an A, a QuadraTile, an A, an 8º, an A, three SuperDuos, and three 15ºs, and sew through the available hole of the last SuperDuo **(figure 2)**. Getting this pattern is important.

hint You can use two colors of 15ºs in the end picot.

3. Pick up a SuperDuo, and sew through the available hole of the next SuperDuo **(figure 3)**. Pull tight to take up any slack.

4. Pick up an A, an 8º, and an A, and sew through the available hole of the QuadraTile that is adjacent to the hole sewn through in the previous step **(figure 4)**. Pick up an A, an 8º, an A, and sew through the corresponding hole of the next QuadraTile. Pick up an A, an 8º, and an A, and sew through the available hole of the next Super-Duo **(figure 5)**. Pick up a SuperDuo, and sew through the available hole of the next SuperDuo **(figure 6)**.

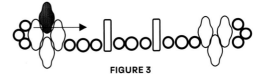

FIGURE 2

FIGURE 3

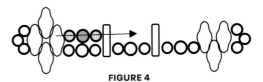

FIGURE 4

FIGURE 5

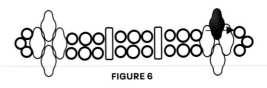

FIGURE 6

5. Retrace the thread path through the three 15ºs and the next two SuperDuos. Turn and sew through the available hole of the SuperDuo your thread is exiting as shown in **figure 7**. Rotate your work so the needle is at the top of your work surface.

6. Pick up a SuperDuo and three 15ºs, and sew through the available hole of the same SuperDuo **(figure 8)**.

7. Pick up two SuperDuos, an A, an 8º, an A, a QuadraTile, an A, an 8º, an A, a QuadraTile, an A, an 8º, an A, three SuperDuos, and three 15ºs. Sew through the available hole of the last SuperDuo. Sew through the available hole of the SuperDuo added in step 3 and the available hole of the first SuperDuo in the three-SuperDuo set picked up in this step, flipping the middle SuperDuo over **(figure 9)**.

8. Pick up an A, 8º, and an A, and sew through the corresponding hole of the QuadraTile on the new unit. Repeat this stitch, and then pick up an A, an 8º, and an A, and sew through the available hole of the next SuperDuo, the available hole of the "flipped over" SuperDuo added in the previous step, and the corresponding hole of the next SuperDuo **(figure 10)**. Retrace the thread path through the three 15ºs and the next two SuperDuos. Turn and sew through the available hole of the SuperDuo your thread is exiting (highlighted red) **(figure 11)**.

FIGURE 7

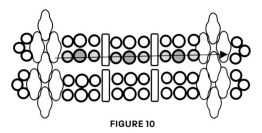

FIGURE 8

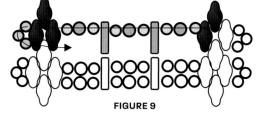

FIGURE 9

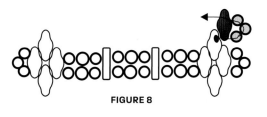

FIGURE 10

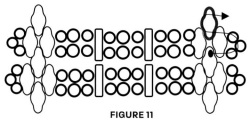

FIGURE 11

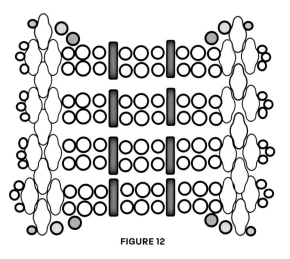

FIGURE 12

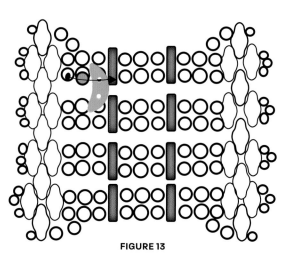

FIGURE 13

9. Repeat steps 6–8 to the desired length, ending and adding thread as needed. You must have an even number of units. With the thread exiting the middle protruding SuperDuo, pick up a 15º, and sew back through the SuperDuo. Pick up a color B 11º seed bead and an A, and sew through the 8º in the last row. Continue through all the beads in the last row, and repeat this step on the other edge (**figure 12**). Sew through the beadwork and repeat for all four corners.

10. With the needle pointing toward the center of the beadwork, sew through the beads in the second row from an end to exit the first A heading toward the QuadraTile. Pick up a B and a Crescent bead, and sew through the corresponding available hole of the QuadraTile (**figure 13**). Pay special attention to the position of the Crescent bead, and make sure you are sewing through the right hole so the Crescents are positioned as shown in **figure 13**. Pick up a Crescent, a B, and a Crescent, and sew through the corresponding hole of the next QuadraTile (**figure 14**). Pick up a Crescent and a B, and sew through the last A before the next SuperDuo (**figure 15**).

11. Following the thread path shown in figure 16, sew through the beads to exit the A directly beside the A your thread exited at the start of this step. Pick up a B, and sew through the available hole of the Crescent bead and continue through the adjacent hole of the next QuadraTile. Sew through the available hole of the next Crescent, pick up a B, and sew through the available hole of the next Crescent. Continue through the adjacent hole of the QuadraTile, and sew through the available hole of the following Crescent. Pick up a B, and sew through the last A in the row of the base (**figure 16**). This completes a Crescent box row.

12. Sew through the beadwork to exit the first A after a SuperDuo in the sixth row from the end. You are skipping two rows of the A, 8º, and A combination. Work as in steps 10 and 11 to complete another Crescent box row.

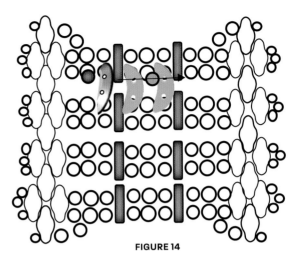

FIGURE 14

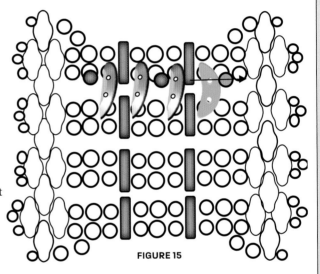

FIGURE 15

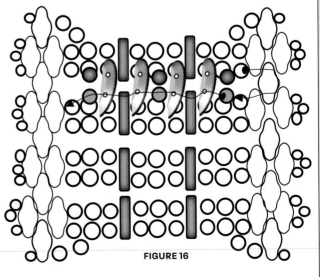

FIGURE 16

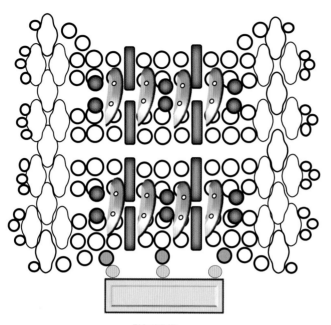

FIGURE 17

13. Continue working as in steps 10–12 to embellish the band with Crescent boxes.

14. Add a clasp: Sew through the beadwork to exit an 8º in an end row of the base. Pick up one or two 11ºs and one half of the clasp, and then sew back through the 11º(s) and the 8º in the base **(figure 17)**. Repeat to connect the remaining loops, and retrace the thread path several times to reinforce the connection. End the working thread. Remove the stop bead and attach a needle to the tail. Repeat this step for the other half of the clasp.

Marcia's Tip

In some beadwork projects, you can take twice the amount of thread you are comfortable working with and wind half of it on a spool or other storage device for use later. This is great for projects that are worked first and then embellished—or worked in two directions.

Thread your needle with about 4–6 yd. (3.7–5.5m). This technique allows you to take more thread than you would normally want to work with and "park" it on a storage device to set aside for later when you run out of thread. Find the halfway point of the thread, and wrap from that midpoint around your storage device. This will also act as a stop bead. When you are low on thread, unwrap the thread, place your needle on that end, and continue to sew. This technique cuts down on adding thread. I call this spooling off. (Note: It does not work in all designs and not at all in herringbone. There is a fan-out effect in herringbone that will be interrupted if you go in two directions.)

intermediate

little lifeboats bracelet

This project is built one section at a time for the length—then, you will add a second layer on top. I love the way the sections look like tiny, nautical floats!

Supplies

- **15–21** 4mm fire-polished or round beads
- **112–160** 3mm melon, round, or fire-polished beads
- **14–20** CzechMate Tile beads
- **28–40** SuperDuo beads
- 5g 11º seed beads
- 5g 15º seed beads
- Scissors
- Beading needle, size 11
- Fireline, 6-lb. test, or thread of your choice
- Stop bead
- Spool (optional)
- Two-hole clasp

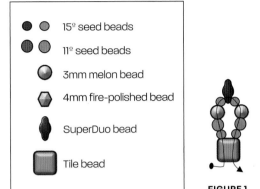

- 15º seed beads
- 11º seed beads
- 3mm melon bead
- 4mm fire-polished bead
- SuperDuo bead
- Tile bead

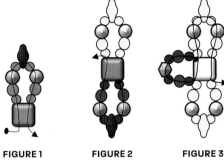

FIGURE 1   FIGURE 2   FIGURE 3

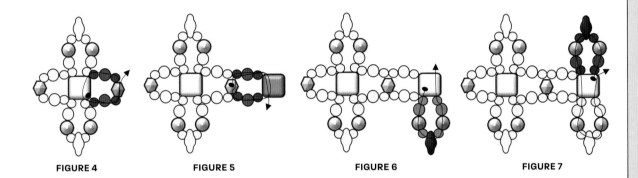

FIGURE 4   FIGURE 5   FIGURE 6   FIGURE 7

MAKE THE BRACELET

1. Thread a needle on the longest piece of thread you are comfortable using (see "Marcia's Tip," p. 46).

2. Pick up a Tile bead, a 15º seed bead, an 11º seed bead, a 3mm melon bead, a 15º, a SuperDuo bead, a 15º, a 3mm, an 11º, and a 15º, and sew through the available hole of the Tile (**figure 1**), leaving a 6-in. (15cm) tail. Pick up a 15º, an 11º, a 3mm, a 15º, a SuperDuo, a 15º, a 3mm, an 11º, and a 15º, and sew back through the first hole of the Tile (**figure 2**).

3. Next, you will build "wings" on the Tile. Pick up a 15º, an 11º, a 15º, a 4mm fire-polished bead, a 15º, an 11º, and a 15º. Sew through the Tile again in the same direction. Continue through the first nine beads picked up in step 2 and the adjacent hole of the Tile (**figure 3**).

4. Pick up a 15º, an 11º, a 15º, a 4mm, a 15º, an 11º, and a 15º. Sew through the nearest hole of the Tile again in the same direction, and continue through the first four beads picked up in this step to exit the 4mm (**figure 4**).

5. Pick up a 15º, an 11º, a 15º, a Tile, a 15º, an 11º, and a 15º, and sew back through the 4mm in the same direction. Continue through the first four beads picked up in this step to exit the Tile (**figure 5**).

6. The SuperDuo loops are next: Pick up a 15º, an 11º, a 3mm, a 15º, a SuperDuo, a 15º, a 3mm, an 11º, and a 15º, and sew through the opposite hole of the Tile (**figure 6**). Repeat this stitch to create a SuperDuo loop on the other side of the Tile. Continue through the first 10 beads picked up in this step to exit the Tile (**figure 7**).

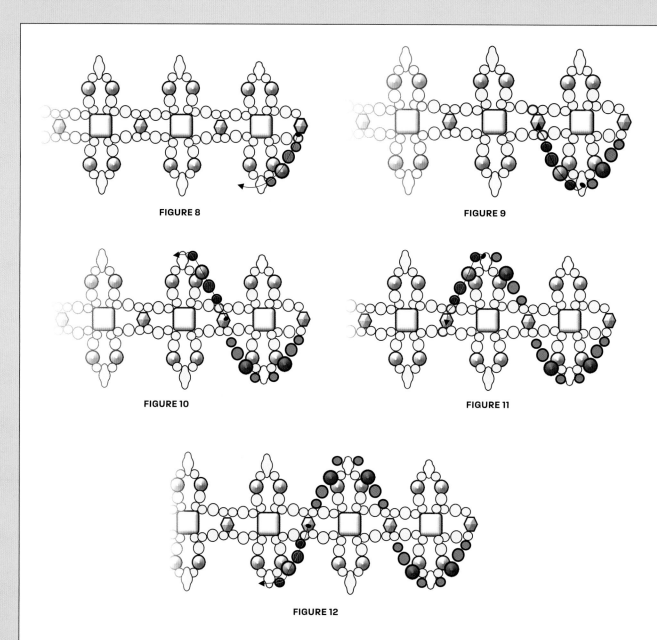

FIGURE 8

FIGURE 9

FIGURE 10

FIGURE 11

FIGURE 12

7. Work as in steps 4–6 to the desired length, ending with a 4mm on the edge, ending and adding thread as needed (this piece will shrink about ½ in./1.3cm when you add the next layer).

8. With your thread exiting an end 4mm, sew through the adjacent 15º (highlighted red) and pick up a 15º, an 11º, a 3mm, and a 15º, and sew through the available hole of the nearest SuperDuo **(figure 8)**. Pull so the SuperDuos are standing up. (The direction you bead at the start of the pattern, pointing up or down, will depend on the number of units you built.)

9. Work toward the tail to make continuing units: Pick up a 15º, a 3mm, an 11º, and a 15º, and sew through the 15º, 4mm, and 15º (highlighted red) **(figure 9)**. Your thread has crossed the original band and is exiting a 15º on the opposite edge. Pick up a 15º, an 11º, a 3mm, and a 15º, and sew through the available hole of the next SuperDuo **(figure 10)**. You are going to continue the alternating pattern, traveling in a zig-zag pattern **(figure 11)**. This is a slightly different reversing pattern, so pay attention **(figures 12–14)**.

10. With your thread exiting the last SuperDuo in the band, pick up a 15º, a 3mm, an 11º, and a 15º, and sew

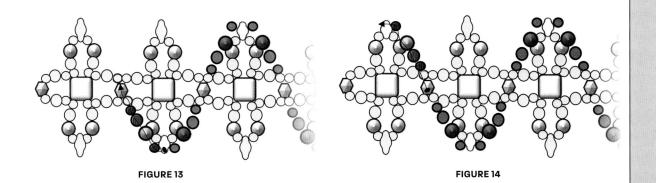

FIGURE 13

FIGURE 14

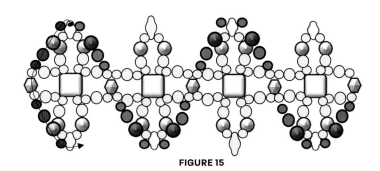

FIGURE 15

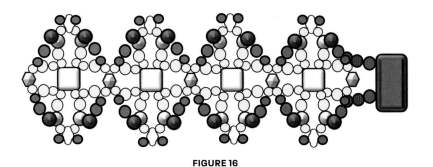

FIGURE 16

through the end 15º, 4mm, and 15º. Pick up a 15º, an 11º, a 3mm, and a 15º, and sew through the available hole of the SuperDuo opposite the one your thread exited at the start of this step **(figure 15)**.

11. Repeat the alternating pattern back to the other end of the bracelet. With the thread exiting the last SuperDuo, continue through the adjacent 15º, 3mm, and 11º to be in position to attach the clasp.

12. Pick up one or two 11ºs and the loop of one half of a two-strand clasp. Sew back through the 11ºs picked up

in this step and the 11º your thread exited at the start of this step, with the needle pointing toward the opposite edge of the bracelet. Retrace the thread path several times to reinforce, and then sew through the beadwork to exit the corresponding 11º on the opposite side of the bracelet. Again, your needle should be pointing toward the opposite edge. Repeat this step to attach the remaining loop of the clasp **(figure 16)**. End the working thread. Thread a needle on the tail, and repeat this step to attach the other half of the clasp.

golden crescent bracelet

There's a hidden bit of magic in this project construction: You are going to be making five passes back and forth along the length of the bracelet. The final step will pop the Crescent bead right into place.

Supplies
- **18–26** 6mm fire-polished or round beads
- **40–56** 3mm rondelle beads
- **44–56** 3mm fire-polished beads
- **10-14** Crescent beads
- **20–28** Bar beads
- **11–15** QuadraTile beads
- 10g 11º seed beads
- 5g 15º seed beads
- Scissors
- Beading needle, size 11
- Fireline, 6-lb. test, or thread of your choice
- Pin or awl
- Clasp

MAKE THE BRACELET

1. Thread a needle on a comfortable length of thread (see "Marcia's Tip," p. 46).

2. Turn 1: These beads will serve as your "stop" beads: Pick up three 11º seed beads and a QuadraTile bead. Sew back through any available hole in the QuadraTile, and continue through the 11ºs and back through the QuadraTile **(figure 1)**.

3. Row 1: Pick up a 15º seed bead, an 11º, a 15º, an 11º, a 15º, a Bar bead, a 15º, an 11º, a 15º, an 11º, a 15º, and a QuadraTile. Repeat this pattern to the desired length, ending with a QuadraTile **(figure 2)**. You can adjust the length slightly with 11ºs when adding the clasp.

4. Turn 2: Pick up three 11ºs, and work as in Turn 1 using two holes of the QuadraTile to secure the tension. Sew through the available hole of the QuadraTile that is adjacent to the hole sewn through in the previous step **(figure 3)**. This will form the bottom base of the bracelet.

5. Row 2: To add beads between the QuadraTiles, pick up a 15º, an 11º, a 15º, an 11º, a 15º, a Bar bead, a 15º, an 11º, a 15º, an 11º, and a 15º, and sew through the QuadraTile **(figure 4)**. Make sure you are sewing through the same hole in each QuadraTile to keep them all aligned properly.

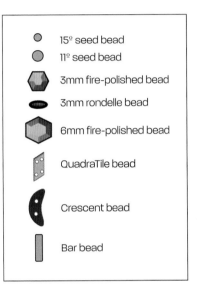

●	15º seed bead
●	11º seed bead
⬡	3mm fire-polished bead
⬭	3mm rondelle bead
⬡	6mm fire-polished bead
▮	QuadraTile bead
◖	Crescent bead
▮	Bar bead

FIGURE 1

FIGURE 2

FIGURE 3

FIGURE 4

6. Turn 3: Pick up three 11°s, and sew through the corresponding available hole in the QuadraTile. Work as in Turn 1, sewing through the QuadraTile and the 11°s to secure and exit a top hole in the QuadraTile (**figure 5**).

7. Row 3: Pick up an 11°, a 3mm fire-polished bead, bead, an 11°, a 15°, a Crescent bead, a 15°, an 11°, a 3mm fire-polished, and an 11°, and sew through the corresponding hole of the next QuadraTile (**figure 6**). Repeat for the length of the bracelet (**figure 7**).

hint **When you pick up the Crescents, point them downward. The beads will not seem to fit right at this point.**

8. Turn 4 and Row 4: Pick up three 11°s, and sew through the remaining available hole of the QuadraTile. Work as in Turn 1 to secure. Fill in the 11°s and 3mm

fire-polished beads as in step 7, matching the other side, being sure to sew through the Crescents and QuadraTiles (**figure 8**).

9. Row 5: (Note: **figures 9 and 10** show the base rows created in steps 2–5 without the top just completed in step 7.) With the thread exiting a lower hole in the QuadraTile, pick up a 15°, an 11°, a 3mm fire-polished bead, an 11°, and a 15°, and sew through the second hole of the Bar (**figure 9**). Then pick up an 11°, a 15°, an 11°, a 6mm fire-polished bead, an 11°, a 15°, and an 11°, and sew through the next Bar. Repeat the fill-in from Bar to Bar with the 6mm-seed bead combination. At the end, pick up a 15°, an 11°, a 3mm fire-polished, an 11°, and a 15°, and sew through the lower hole of the QuadraTile (**figure 10**).

10. Row 6: Sew through the beadwork to the other side and repeat step 9 (Row 5) (**figure 11**).

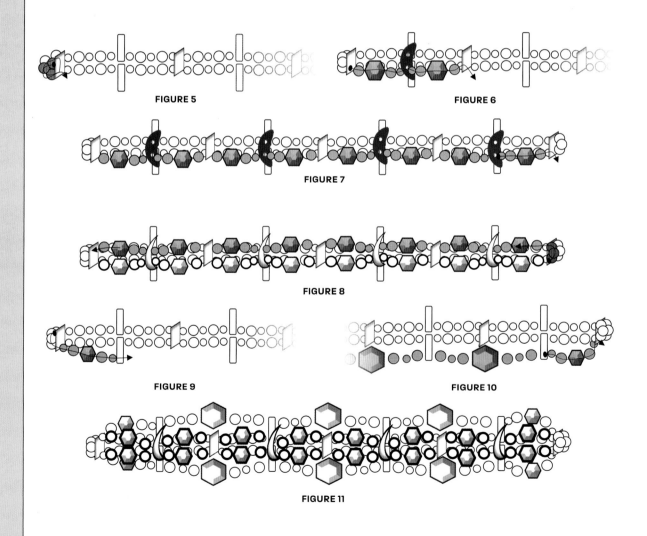

FIGURE 5

FIGURE 6

FIGURE 7

FIGURE 8

FIGURE 9

FIGURE 10

FIGURE 11

11. Sew through the beadwork to exit the first 3mm fire-polished bead on the bottom. Pick up a 15º, a 3mm rondelle bead, an 11º, and a 15º, and sew through the Crescent **(figure 12)**. Pick up a 15º, an 11º, a rondelle, and a 15º, and sew through the 11º, 6mm, and 11º **(figure 13)**. Repeat, alternating these two bead patterns, to the end. Sew through the beadwork to the other side, and repeat this step.

12. Please read this whole paragraph before you add the bead to the bracelet! Sew through the beadwork along the previous row to exit the 11º after the 3mm. (All the 11ºs are highlighted red in the illustration.) Pick up a 15º, and sew through the next 11º and 3mm from the

back side of the bracelet. This pops up the Crescent and places the 15º under the Crescent **(figure 14)**. You cannot see it; it is functional, not visible. You must work the thread under the Crescent with a needle, pin, or awl. This is the magic step that makes the whole piece work right. Repeat for the length of bracelet. Sew through the beadwork to the other side of the piece, and repeat on the other side.

13. Attach a clasp. The clasp can be built out from the QuadraTile on the end. There are two point beads from the two picots at the end of the QuadraTile. Add to the length on those two picot beads by adding beads one at a time between the point beads **(figures 15 and 16)**.

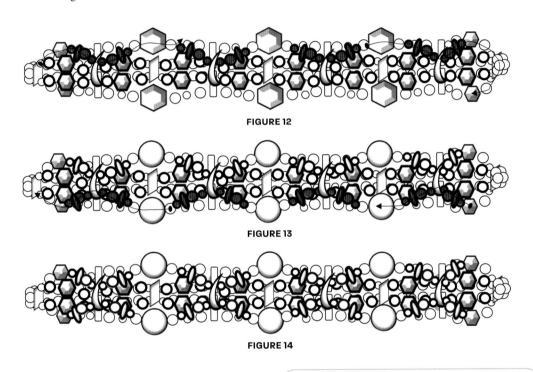

FIGURE 12

FIGURE 13

FIGURE 14

FIGURE 15

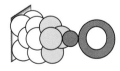

FIGURE 16

Marcia's Tip

Do not try to back out twice! It is best to take off the needle to rip out your work, but if you do sew backwards—definitely, do NOT try twice! You will probably put a knot in the middle of the inside of a bead, which is almost impossible to get out—and fixing your work may require cutting the thread. It will take less time to re-thread a needle than to take out knots.

bubbles bracelet

This project is built one section at a time. A blue-and-black color combination makes the bracelet truly shine on your wrist.

Supplies

- **34–38** 5mm melon beads
- 3mm fire-polished beads: **48–60** color A, **34–38** color B
- **17–19** two-hole Cabochon beads
- 5g 11º seed beads in each of **2** colors: A, B
- 5g 15º seed beads
- Two-hole clasp
- Scissors
- Beading needles, size 12 and 13
- Fireline, 6-lb. test, or thread of your choice

MAKE THE BRACELET

1. Thread a needle on the longest piece of thread you are comfortable using (see "Marcia's Tip," p. 46).

2. Pick up a Cabochon bead, a 15º seed bead, a 3mm fire-polished bead, and a 15º, and sew through the available hole of the Cabochon (**figure 1**), leaving a 6-in. (15cm) tail. Pick up a 15º, a 3mm, and a 15º, and sew back through the first hole of the Cabochon and the adjacent 15º to step up (**figure 2**).

3. To make the first "wing" pattern, pick up a 15º, a color A 11º seed bead, a 3mm, an A, and a 15º, and sew through the 15º, Cabochon, 15º, 3mm, 15º, and the other hole of the Cabochon. Sew through the beadwork to exit the next 15º as shown (**figures 3 and 4**).

4. Work as in step 3 to make the other wing (**figure 5**). Sew through the beadwork to exit the 3mm to step up for the outer loop (**figure 6**).

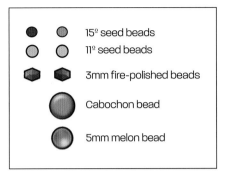

● ●	15º seed beads	
○ ○	11º seed beads	
⬡ ⬡	3mm fire-polished beads	
●	Cabochon bead	
●	5mm melon bead	

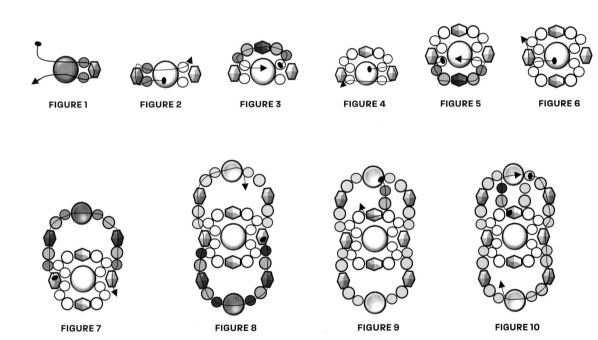

FIGURE 1   **FIGURE 2**   **FIGURE 3**   **FIGURE 4**   **FIGURE 5**   **FIGURE 6**

FIGURE 7   **FIGURE 8**   **FIGURE 9**   **FIGURE 10**

5. To make the outer loops: Pick up a 15º, a color B 11º seed bead, a 3mm, an A, a 15º, a 5mm melon bead, a 15º, a B, a 3mm, an A, and a 15º, and sew through the opposite 3mm **(figure 7)**. Repeat the outer loop pattern on the other side, and sew through the first loop to exit the 5mm **(figure 8)**. The loops are floppy at this point.

6. To connect the outer 5mm to the inner 3mm: With the thread exiting the 5mm, pick up a 15º and an A, and sew through the 3mm on this side **(figure 9)**. Pick up an A and a 15º, and sew through the outer 5mm in the same direction. Sew through the beadwork to exit the 5mm on the opposite side of your work **(figure 10)**.

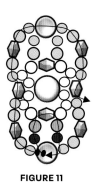

FIGURE 11

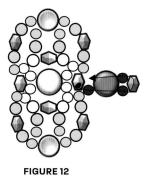

FIGURE 12

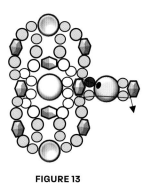

FIGURE 13

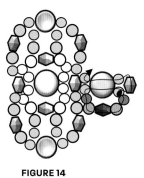

FIGURE 14

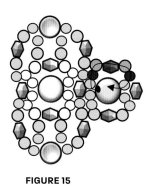

FIGURE 15

7. Work as in step 6 on this side. Sew through the beadwork to exit the 3mm picked up in step 2 (highlighted red) **(figure 11)**. This is the first unit; additional units have shared beads.

8. Continuing units: Pick up a 15º, a Cabochon, a 15º, a 3mm, and a 15º, and sew through the available hole of the Cabochon **(figure 12)**. Pick up a 15º, and sew through the 3mm that is shared with the previous unit (highlighted red). Sew back through the 15º, Cabochon, and 15º **(figure 13)**.

9. Make the inner loop: Pick up a 15º, an A, a 3mm, an A, and a 15º, and sew through the 15º on the other side of the Cabochon. Continue through the Cabochon, 15º, and the other hole of the Cabochon to exit the 15º on the other side **(figure 14)**.

10. Work as in step 9 to make the second loop **(figure 15)**. Step up for the outer loop by exiting a 3mm (highlighted red) **(figure 16)**.

11. Make the outer loop: Pick up a B, a 15º, a 5mm, a 15º, a B, a 3mm, a B, and a 15º, and sew through a 3mm (highlighted red) **(figure 17)**.

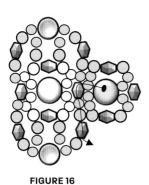

FIGURE 16

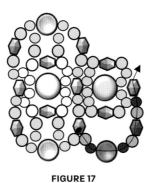

FIGURE 17

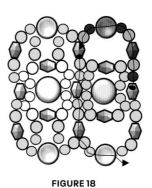

FIGURE 18

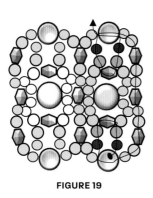

FIGURE 19

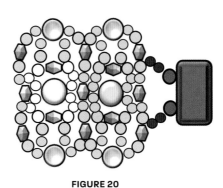

FIGURE 20

12. Make the second outer loop: Pick up a 15º, a B, a 3mm, a B, a 15º, a 5mm, a 15º, and a B, and sew through the 3mm shared with the previous unit (highlighted red) **(figure 18)**. Sew through the beadwork to exit a 5mm on the outer edge.

13. Work as in steps 6 and 7 **(figure 19)**, ending and adding thread as needed. If you find that your beads at the joint near the Cabochon are tight, you may need to switch to a size 13 needle.

14. Sew through the beadwork to exit a side 3mm, and repeat steps 8–13 until you reach the desired length.

15. Sew through the beadwork to exit an 3mm in the outer loop in the end unit. Pick up two seed beads, and sew through one loop of the clasp. Sew back through the seed beads, and sew through the beads to retrace the thread path several times to secure. Continue through the beads at the end of the bracelet to exit the corresponding seed bead in the other outer loop. Repeat this step to attach the other loop of the clasp **(figure 20)**. End the working thread. Attach a needle to the tail, and repeat on the other end.

chunky monkey bracelet

Using Crescent beads and a double layer of beads creates this chunky, stylish bracelet.

Supplies

- **7** (**1** per unit) 8mm round, fire-polished, or crystal round beads
- **70** (**10** per unit) 3mm or 4mm round or fire-polished beads
- **84** (**12** per unit) Crescent beads (**2** colors, if desired)
- **238** (**34** per unit) SuperDuo beads
- 5g 11º seed beads
- 5g 15º seed beads
- Two-hole clasp
- Scissors
- Beading needles, size 11 or 12
- Fireline, 6-lb. test, or thread of your choice
- Stop bead (optional)

NOTE: *Mini SuperDuos will work with 3mm round or fire-polished beads.*

MAKE THE BRACELET

1. Thread a needle on 30 in. (76cm) of thread, and attach a stop bead, leaving a 6-in. (15cm) tail. This makes one unit; each unit is stitched and joined separately. Pick up an 8mm round bead and a SuperDuo bead, and sew back through the 8mm (**figure 1**).

2. Pick up a SuperDuo, and sew back through the 8mm, the first SuperDuo, and the 8mm again. Pull snug to take up any slack, and tie a knot with the working thread and the tail. Continue through the SuperDuo (**figure 2**).

FIGURE 1   FIGURE 2   FIGURE 3   FIGURE 4   FIGURE 5

hint **If you are likely to have a problem seeing which SuperDuo is at the top and bottom, you may use two colors to help you see the pattern.**

3. Pick up a repeating pattern of an 11º seed bead and a SuperDuo four times, and then pick up an 11º. Sew through the SuperDuo on the opposite side **(figure 3)**. These beads will form a loop around one half of the 8mm. Repeat to create a loop around the other half of the 8mm. Then, with the thread exiting the second SuperDuo added in step 2, repeat this step again to add a double layer of SuperDuos and 11ºs. These loops will sit on top of the first two loops **(figures 4 and 5)**.

●	15º seed bead
○	11º seed bead
⬡	4mm fire-polished bead
⬭	SuperDuo bead
◗	Crescent bead
⬤	8mm round bead

FIGURE 6 **FIGURE 7** **FIGURE 8** **FIGURE 9**

FIGURE 10 **FIGURE 11** **FIGURE 12**

4. Turn to exit the available hole of the nearest Super-Duo added in step 2. Pick up a SuperDuo and a 15º seed bead, and sew through the next SuperDuo in the top layer (**figure 6**). Pick up a 15º, a SuperDuo, and a 15º, and sew through the next SuperDuo. Repeat twice. For the fourth repeat, pick up a 15º and a SuperDuo, and sew through the other SuperDuo added in step 2 (**figure 7**). Repeat for the other side of the 8mm (**figure 8**).

5. Sew through the first hole of the first new SuperDuo added. Pick up a 15º, and sew through the nearest hole of the next SuperDuo in the second ring of SuperDuos (**figure 9**).

6. Pick up a 15º, a SuperDuo, and a 15º, and sew through the nearest hole of the next SuperDuo (**figure 10**). Repeat twice. Pick up a 15º, and continue to the other side by sewing through the next three SuperDuos (**figure 11**).

7. Pick up a 15º, and sew through the next SuperDuo in the top layer of SuperDuos. Repeat step 6 (**figure 12**).

8. Turn and sew through the available hole of the Super-Duo your thread is exiting. Pick up a 4mm fire-polished bead, and sew through the available hole of the next SuperDuo. Pick up a 15º, a 4mm, and a 15º, and sew through the available hole of the next SuperDuo. Pick up three Crescent beads, and sew through the available hole of the next SuperDuo. Pick up three Crescents, and sew through the available hole of the next SuperDuo. Pick up a 15º, a 4mm, and a 15º, and sew through the available hole of the next SuperDuo (**figure 13**).

9. Work as in step 8 to embellish the other side of the ring (**figure 14**).

10. Sew through the beadwork to exit the SuperDuo after the center 4mm (highlighted red). Pick up a 15º, a 4mm, and a 15º, and sew through the available holes of the next three Crescents. Sew through the next outer hole of the SuperDuo, the available hole of the next three Crescents, and the outer hole of the SuperDuo. Repeat, and sew through the beadwork to exit the SuperDuo after the next center 4mm (**figure 15**).

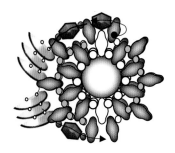

FIGURE 13

Marcia's Tip

To get the best tension on your work, learn to pull straight out from the bead hole. This will both protect the thread from stress and help you to get your beadwork tighter. Just pay some attention to the way the hole is facing, and you will improve your beading.

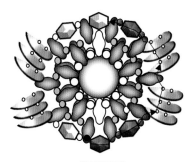

FIGURE 14

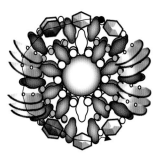

FIGURE 15

FIGURE 16

FIGURE 17

11. Work as in step 10 to complete the other half of the ring (**figure 16**). End the tail, but not the working thread, and set aside. This completes one unit.

12. To make the second unit of the bracelet, follow steps 1–7. At step 8, sew through a 4mm on the end of the first bracelet unit and continue the steps as before from step 8 (**figure 17**). The only shared bead is the end 4mm. Reinforce this connection. Repeat to make the desired number of units.

13. Attach the clasp: Exit a SuperDuo on the end of the bracelet, with the needle pointing away from center, and pick up one or two 11ºs and one half of the clasp. Sew back through the 11ºs, and continue through the SuperDuo, end 4mm, and next SuperDuo. Pick up the same number of 11ºs, and sew through the second hole of the clasp. Sew back through the 11ºs. Retrace the thread path to reinforce, and end the working thread. Thread a needle on the tail, and repeat to add the other half of the clasp to the other end of the bracelet. End the thread.

secret garden necklace

Combine SuperDuo beads with seed beads, crystals, fire-polished beads, and a cabochon to create this attractive pendant or necklace.

Supplies

- **3** (**1** for a small pendant) 18mm or 24mm cabochons
- **66–70** (**8** for a small pendant) 4mm fire-polished beads
- **58–66** (**8** for a small pendant) 3mm bicone crystals
- **126–130** (**24** for a small pendant) Super Duo beads
- 4g 11º seed beads in **2** colors: A, B
- 4g 15º seed beads
- Box clasp
- Scissors
- Beading needles, size 11 or 12
- Fireline, 6-lb. test, or thread of your choice

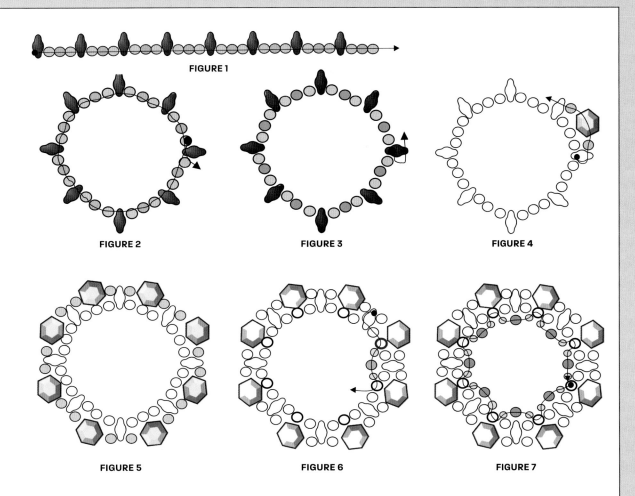

FIGURE 1

FIGURE 2   **FIGURE 3**   **FIGURE 4**

FIGURE 5   **FIGURE 6**   **FIGURE 7**

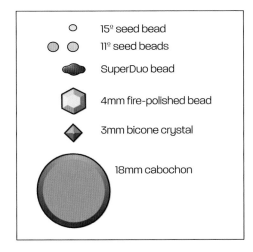

○   15º seed bead

◐ ◑   11º seed beads

      SuperDuo bead

      4mm fire-polished bead

      3mm bicone crystal

      18mm cabochon

tip **You can use a 24mm cabochon, if you like. The number of beads changes from eight SuperDuo beads to 10 SuperDuo beads (adjust all bead numbers to match).**

MAKE THE UNITS

1. Thread a needle on 2 yd. (1.8m) of thread. Pick up a repeating pattern of a SuperDuo bead, a color A 11º seed bead, a color B 11º seed bead, and an A eight times for a total of 32 beads **(figure 1)**. Sew through all the beads again to secure, leaving an 8-in. (20cm) tail. Tie an overhead knot with the working thread and tail **(figure 2)**. Retrace the thread path to reinforce the round, exiting a SuperDuo. Turn and sew through the available hole of the same SuperDuo your thread is exiting **(figure 3)**.

2. Pick up an A, a 4mm fire-polished bead, and an A, and sew through the available hole of the next Super-Duo **(figure 4)**. Repeat to finish the round **(figure 5)**.

3. Sew through the beadwork to exit the original hole of the first SuperDuo picked up in step 1. Continue through the next A and B (highlighted red), and pick up a 15º, a B, and a 15º, and sew through the following B from step 1 **(figure 6)**. Repeat to finish the round (you are working on the back) **(figure 7)**.

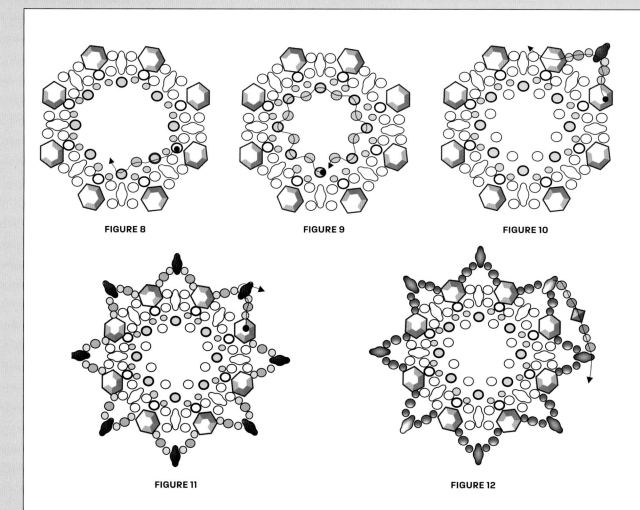

FIGURE 8   **FIGURE 9**   **FIGURE 10**

FIGURE 11   **FIGURE 12**

4. Sew through the beadwork to exit the B just added (highlighted red). Pick up an A, and sew through the next B **(figure 8)**. Repeat to complete the round **(figure 9)**. Pull tight.

5. Sew through the beadwork to exit a 4mm. You will now be working on the front. Pick up 15º, an A, a 15º, a SuperDuo, a 15º, an A, and a 15º, and sew through the next 4mm **(figure 10)**. Repeat to complete the round, and step up through the first four beads picked up in this step to exit a SuperDuo. Turn and sew through the available hole of the same SuperDuo to be in position for the next step **(figure 11)**.

6. Pick up an A, a 15º, a B, a 3mm crystal, a B, a 15º, and an A, and sew through the available hole of the next SuperDuo **(figure 12)**. Repeat to complete the round **(figure 13)**. Sew through the beadwork to exit a 4mm picked up in step 2.

7. Working on the back of the piece, pick up a 15º, and sew through the next A, the top hole of the next SuperDuo, and the following A (highlighted red) **(figure 14)**. Pick up a 15º, and sew through the next 4mm. This will pull the outer ring with the crystal in tight, flipping the SuperDuo in to touch the one hugging the cabochon **(figure 15)**. Repeat to complete the round, and exit a 4mm.

8. This will now be the front of the piece. Pick up an A, a SuperDuo, and an A, and sew through the next 4mm (these beads will hide the back row) **(figure 16)**. Repeat to complete the round.

9. Sew through the beadwork to exit the available hole of the SuperDuo added in the previous step. Pick up a 15º, an A, a B, an A, and a 15º, and sew through the available hole of the next SuperDuo **(figure 17)**. Repeat to complete the round.

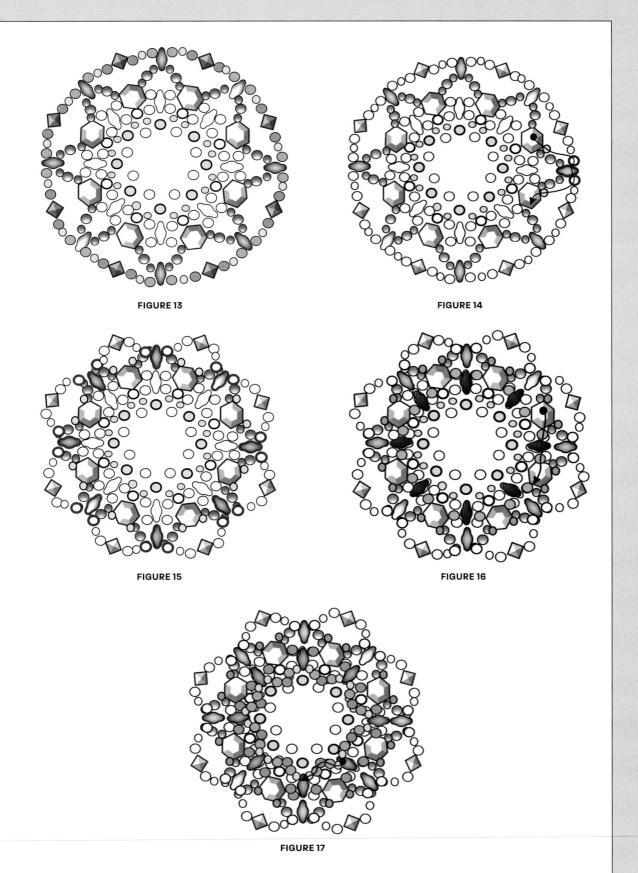

FIGURE 13

FIGURE 14

FIGURE 15

FIGURE 16

FIGURE 17

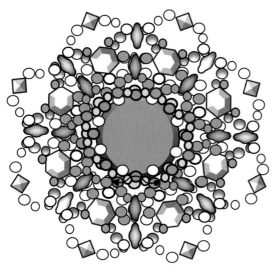

FIGURE 18

10. Place the cabochon in the beadwork. Sew through the beadwork to exit the B from the previous step (highlighted red). Pick up a 15º, a B, and a 15º, and sew through the next B **(figure 18)**. Repeat to complete the round, and then retrace the thread path through the beads in this round to secure the cabochon in the beadwork. End the tail, but not the working thread. This completes one unit.

11. Work as in steps 1–10 for the desired number of units (mine has three). A larger cabochon unit for the center works nicely (see tip). You could also use a larger unit as a nice pendant or single piece for a necklace.

CONNECT THE UNITS

12. Many connections are possible, and the shape of your necklace can vary. I encourage you to get creative! This simple connection joins pairs of crystals on two units. Using the working thread from one unit, sew through the beadwork to exit a crystal along the outer edge. Pick up a 15º, a crystal, and a 15º, and sew through a corresponding crystal on a second unit to connect. Pick up a 15º, a crystal, and a 15º, and sew back through the crystal on the first unit in the same direction. Reinforce each connection. Sew through the beadwork to the next crystal on the first unit, and repeat this step to connect to the corresponding crystal on the second unit. End the working thread. Other bead combinations to attach to the base are possible;

just be sure to use something between the crystals. Add more crystals or seed beads as needed for a lovely drape.

MAKE NECK STRAPS

13. Attach a comfortable length of thread to an end unit, and exit a crystal at the point where you want the neck strap to attach. Pick up a repeating pattern of a 15º, an 11º in the color desired, a 4mm, an 11º, a 15º, a SuperDuo, a 15º, an 11º, a crystal, an 11º, a 15º, and a SuperDuo for the desired length of the neck strap. Attach a clasp now, if you like (see step 14), or simply retrace the pattern, minus the SuperDuo, sewing through the available hole of the SuperDuo on the return path. Reinforce the thread path through all the beads in the neck strap to secure. Make a second neck strap.

14. To connect the clasp, exit an end SuperDuo, pick up four 11ºs (either color) and the clasp, and sew back through the last 11º added. Pick up three 11ºs, and sew through the available hole of the SuperDuo. Repeat on the other end of the necklace to attach the other half of the clasp. End the threads.

persian rug bracelet

Use QuadraTiles to make this densely layered cuff. In either jewel tones or contrasting colors, this is a real statement piece!

FIGURE 1 **FIGURE 2** **FIGURE 3**

FIGURE 4 **FIGURE 5**

FIGURE 6 **FIGURE 7**

FIGURE 8 **FIGURE 9**

Supplies

- **38–50** 5mm melon beads
- **40–52** 4mm bicone crystals
- **80–108** 3mm fire-polished beads
- **38–50** 2mm round beads
- **60–88** QuadraTile beads
- **80–108** 3x6mm Infinity beads (or Bar beads)
- 5g 11º seed beads in each of **2** colors: A, B
- 5g 15º seed beads
- Multi-hole clasp
- Scissors
- Beading needles, size 11 or 12
- Fireline, 6-lb. test, or thread of your choice

NOTE: Select a thread color that will blend closest to the QuadraTile bead. Pay attention to the orientation of the QuadraTile holes as you work; they flip and twist easily before they are all connected. You will find yourself using the wrong hole if you are not careful. Make sure you are using the correct hole, and you will get much better results.

MAKE THE BRACELET

1. Thread a needle on the longest length of thread you are comfortable using.

2. Pick up QuadraTile bead, a color A 11º seed bead, a color B 11º, and an A, and sew through an available hole of the QuadraTile **(figure 1)**. Secure the thread by sewing through all the beads a second time and exiting the QuadraTile **(figure 2)**.

3. Pick up an A, a B, an A, a 4mm crystal, an A, a B, an A, a QuadraTile, an A, a B, an A, a crystal, an A, a B, an A, a QuadraTile, an A, a B, and an A, and sew back through an adjacent hole of the last QuadraTile picked up **(figure 3)**. Getting this pattern is important. You are using four holes of the QuadraTile as you work each pattern. The crystals are placed on the top at the outer edges only.

4. Pick up a B, an Infinity bead, a 3mm fire-polished bead, an Infinity bead, and a B, and sew through the back or underside of the QuadraTile below the top row **(figure 4)**. Repeat this pattern to the other edge. This

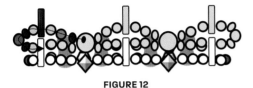

FIGURE 10

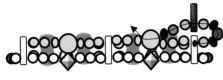

FIGURE 11

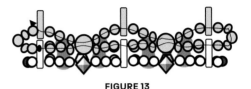

FIGURE 12

FIGURE 13

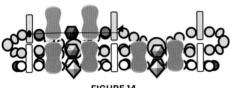

FIGURE 14

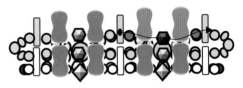

FIGURE 15

row is on the backside just under the top **(figure 5)**. Pay attention to the four holes on the QuadraTile.

5. Sew through an adjacent hole in the QuadraTile to reach the back side. Pick up a B, and sew through the available hole of the next Infinity. Pull snug. Pick up a 3mm, and sew through the available hole of the next Infinity. Pick up a B, and sew through the corresponding hole of the next QuadraTile **(figure 6)**. Pick up a B, and sew through the next Infinity. Pick up a 3mm, and sew through the next Infinity. Pick up a B, and sew through the available hole of the next QuadraTile **(figure 7)**. This finishes the back side of the first unit.

6. Sew through the adjacent hole of the QuadraTile to reach the top front side. Pick up an A, a B, a 15º seed bead, a 5mm melon bead, a 15º, a B, and an A, and sew through the front of the middle QuadraTile **(figure 8)**. Repeat the pattern, sewing through the edge Quadra-Tile. This completes the top of the first unit **(figure 9)**.

7. Pick up an A, a 15º, a 2mm round bead, a 15º, an A, a QuadraTile, an A, a B, and a 15º, and sew through the 5mm picked up in the previous unit **(figure 10)**.

8. Pick up a 15º, a B, an A, a QuadraTile, an A, a B, and a 15º, and sew through the second 5mm picked up in the previous unit **(figure 11)**.

9. Pick up a 15º, a B, an A, a QuadraTile, an A, a 15º, a 2mm, a 15º, and an A, and make a turn by sewing through the QuadraTile picked up in the previous unit back to front with the needle pointing toward the bracelet **(figure 12)**.

10. Sew through the width of the bracelet all around **(figure 13)**.

11. Sew through the beadwork to exit the back side of the QuadraTile under the top just added. Make sure your QuadraTile is positioned correctly. Sew through the available hole directly under the hole you are exiting, pick up a B, an Infinity, a 3mm, an Infinity, and a B, and sew through the back or underside of the QuadraTile below the top row **(figure 14)**. Repeat the pattern to the other edge **(figure 15)**.

12. Pick up an A, a 15º, a 2mm, a 15º, and an A, and make the turn by sewing through the adjacent end QuadraTile in the previous row (you are still on the

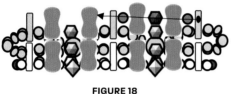

FIGURE 16

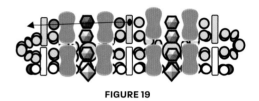

FIGURE 17

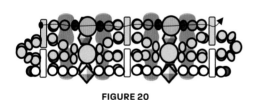

FIGURE 18

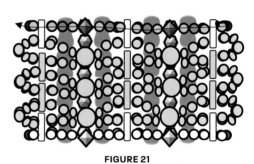

FIGURE 19

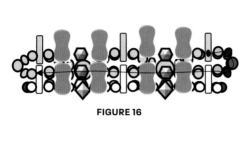

FIGURE 20

FIGURE 21

back). Sew through all the beads in this row to exit the QuadraTile on this end **(figure 16)**. Pick up an A, a 15º, a 3mm, a 15º, and an A, and once again, sew through the bracelet to the other side. Exit through the QuadraTile **(figure 17)**. This step connects the two units on the back side. Both upper and lower sides are now connected.

13. Exit the QuadraTile to the back side. Pick up a B, and sew through an Infinity. Pull snug. Pick up a 3mm, and sew through an Infinity. Pick up a B, and sew through a QuadraTile **(figure 18)**. Pick up a B, and sew through an Infinity. Pick up a 3mm, and sew through an Infinity. Pick up a B, and sew through the corresponding hole of the end QuadraTile **(figure 19)**. You are still working on the back side.

14. Turn and sew through the available hole in the QuadraTile that is above the hole your thread is exiting to be in position to work the front of the bracelet. Pick up an A, a B, a 15º, a 5mm, a 15º, a B, and an A, and sew through the corresponding hole of the next QuadraTile. Repeat the pattern, and exit the corresponding hole of the end QuadraTile **(figure 20)**.

15. Repeat steps 7–14 to the desired length, ending and adding thread as needed. For the last unit: In step 14, replace the 5mm with a crystal to match the starting unit. Sew through the end QuadraTile, pick up an A, a B, and an A, and sew through the corresponding hole of the next QuadraTile **(figure 21)**. Sew through all the beads in this row to the other side, and repeat this step. On average, you will need 20 units with QuadraTiles.

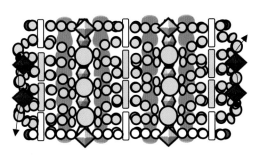

FIGURE 22

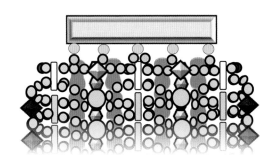

FIGURE 23

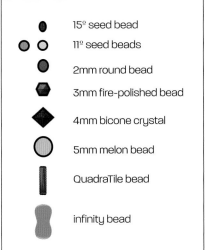

- 15º seed bead
- 11º seed beads
- 2mm round bead
- 3mm fire-polished bead
- 4mm bicone crystal
- 5mm melon bead
- QuadraTile bead
- infinity bead

Marcia's Tip

Allow your beads to fall off the needle onto the thread. So often, I observe students picking up all their beads on the needle and then sewing. Your needle is a slippery surface, and it does not take much of a tilt to make a bead fall off. By allowing your beads to fall onto the thread and down to your work, you lessen the chance you will lose a bead. This tip is most important when you are picking up a lot of beads at one time.

16. Once you have reached the desired length, sew through the beadwork to exit the 15º after the 2mm along the top edge. Pick up a crystal, and sew through the 15º, 2mm, and 15º. Repeat to the end of the bracelet. Sew through the beadwork and repeat on the other side **(figure 22)**.

17. Add seed beads to fit and connect to your clasp shape **(figure 23)**.

curacao bracelet

This bracelet is built one section at a time and joined separately.
Extra beads added with the clasp will allow for movement and comfort.

Supplies

- **36** 6mm round or fire-polished beads
- **18** 4mm fire-polished beads
- **94** 3mm fire-polished or other round, melon, or English-cut beads
- **9** Tile beads
- **36** Triangle beads
- **18** Bar or Brick beads
- **84** 8º seed beads
- 5g 11º seed beads
- 5g 15º seed beads
- Four-hole clasp
- Scissors
- Beading needles, size 12 or 13
- Fireline, 6- or 8-lb. test, or thread of your choice

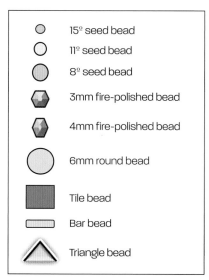

○	15º seed bead
○	11º seed bead
○	8º seed bead
⬡	3mm fire-polished bead
⬡	4mm fire-polished bead
○	6mm round bead
▢	Tile bead
▭	Bar bead
△	Triangle bead

MAKE THE BRACELET

1. Thread the needle on 1 yd. (.9m) of thread.

2. Pick up a Tile bead, a 15º seed bead, an 11º seed bead, a 4mm fire-polished bead, an 11º, and a 15º, and sew through the available hole of the Tile (**figure 1**), leaving a 6-in. (15cm) tail. Pick up a 15º, an 11º, a 4mm, an 11º, and a 15º, and sew back through the first hole of the Tile in the same direction. Sew through the next three beads. Step up through the 4mm (**figure 2**).

3. You'll build two rather large wings around the Tile with a total of 17 beads on each side. Pick up an 11º, a 3mm fire-polished bead, an 11º, a 6mm round bead, an 11º, three 15ºs, a 3mm, three 15ºs, an 11º, a 6mm, an 11º, a 3mm, and an 11º, and sew through the 4mm on the other side of the Tile (**figure 3**). Repeat this step on the other side of the unit. Reinforce the entire loop pattern. Sew through the beadwork to exit the 3mm on the outer edge of the large loop (**figure 4**).

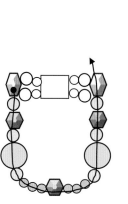

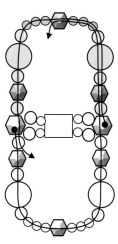

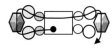

FIGURE 1   **FIGURE 2**   **FIGURE 3**   **FIGURE 4**

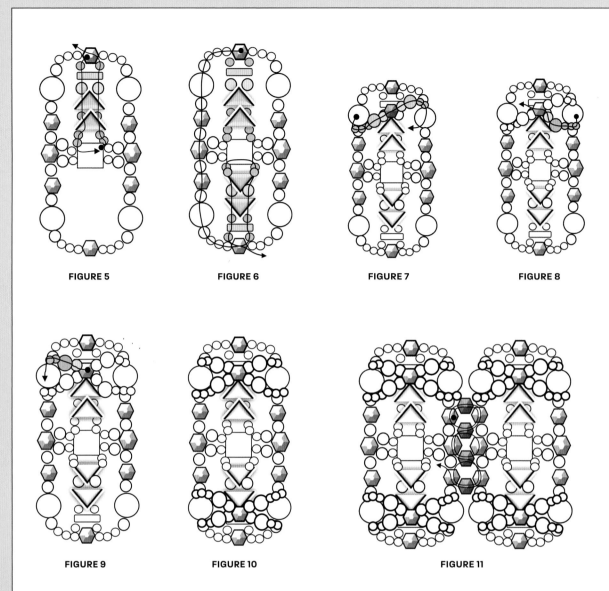

FIGURE 5   **FIGURE 6**   **FIGURE 7**   **FIGURE 8**

FIGURE 9   **FIGURE 10**   **FIGURE 11**

4. You'll connect the outer edge 3mms to the Tiles using Triangle beads. Pick up a 15º, a Bar or Brick bead, an 11º, a Triangle, a 15º, a Triangle, and two 15ºs, and and sew through the next Tile (the number of 15ºs you use to connect to the tile may vary due to the variation in beads, thread and tension). Pick up the matching seed beads to fill the second hole, and sew through the 3mm on the outer wing of beads where you began **(figure 5)**. Reinforce the thread path, if desired.

hint **When using Triangles, double-check that you have the holes aligning so the point is facing the same way.**

5. Sew through the beadwork to exit the opposite 3mm, and repeat the connection of the outer wing of beads to the center Tile, as shown in step 4, to complete the other side **(figure 6)**. Retrace the thread path to reinforce.

6. Sew through the beadwork to exit the 6mm round bead with your needle pointing toward the center of the unit. Pick up a combination to form an "X" shape, connecting from one side to the other over the Bar or Brick. To make this example, pick up three 15ºs, an 8º seed bead, an 11º, a 3mm, an 11º, an 8º, and two 15ºs, and sew through the opposite 6mm **(figure 7)**. Pick up seed beads to match, and sew through the 3mm just added **(figure 8)**. Pick up seed beads to match, and sew

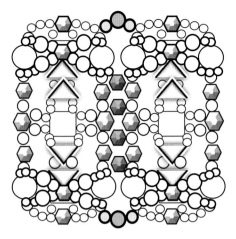

FIGURE 12

Threading a needle can be tricky. When you try to push the thread through the eye of the needle, you may have some difficulty. Instead, think of threading the needle as putting the needle on the thread. Cut the thread with sharp snips on an angle, if possible. Use the cut side of the thread to thread your needle. Hold the thread with its end just barely between your thumb and finger. The little angle of the cut will help as you put your needle on your thread.

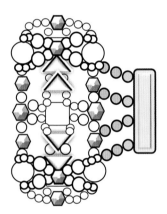

FIGURE 13

through the first 6mm **(figure 9)**. Once you are happy with the combination of your "X" embellishment beads on one side, sew through the beadwork and repeat on the other side **(figure 10)**. Reinforce. (You may complete steps 4 and 6 on the same side before moving to the other side.) End the tail, but not the working thread. This completes the first unit. You will need a total of 7–9 units, depending on the desired length.

7. Using the working thread from one completed unit, connect the units from the 3mms and 4mms on the sides with 3mms between the units **(figure 11)**. There are a total of four 3mms; the center two are shared with the top and bottom boxes. Exit any side 3mm, and pick up a 3mm. Connect to the next unit by sewing through

the 3mm on the new unit. Pick up another 3mm, and connect to the first unit 3mm. Sew around the box, but this time, travel to the 4mm. Pick up a 3mm, and complete that box. Repeat for the third box. Reinforce the connections.

8. Fill in along the edges between the units (or not), depending on your personal taste. Your bead choice will vary slightly. Exit the bead next to the 6mm. Pick up a pleasing combination, such as an 11º, a 4mm, and an 11º, and sew through the corresponding beads on the next unit to bridge that gap **(figure 12)**.

9. Refer to **figure 13** to attach one half of the clasp on each end of the bracelet. End the threads.

dream deep cuff

You'll find yourself dreaming of the many colorful possibilities while you make this beautiful, layered cuff packed with QuadraTile and Tile beads.

Supplies

- **76–92** 4mm round beads
- **76–92** 3mm fire-polished beads
- **36–44** 3mm bicone crystals
- **72–96** Bar or Brick beads
- **19–23** Tile beads
- **38–46** QuadraTile beads
- 7g 11º seed beads
- 5g 15º seed beads
- Three- or four-hole clasp
- Scissors
- Beading needles, size 11 or 12
- Fireline, 6-lb. test, or thread of your choice

NOTE: Select a thread color that will blend closest to the Bar or Brick bead.

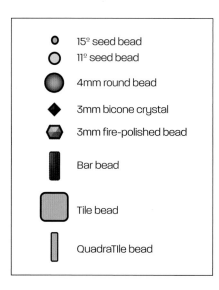

○ 15º seed bead

◯ 11º seed bead

● 4mm round bead

◆ 3mm bicone crystal

⬡ 3mm fire-polished bead

▮ Bar bead

▢ Tile bead

▯ QuadraTile bead

MAKE THE CUFF

1. Thread a needle on the longest thread you are comfortable using (see "Marcia's Tip," p. 46).

2. Pick up a Bar bead and three 11º seed beads, and sew through the available hole of the Bar **(figure 1)**, leaving a 6-in. (15cm) tail. Sew through all the beads a second time to secure.

3. Pick up a Bar, two 11ºs, a 3mm fire-polished bead, an 11º, a QuadraTile bead, a Tile bead, a QuadraTile, an 11º, a 3mm, two 11ºs, two Bars, and three 11ºs, and make the turn by sewing through the available hole of the last Bar picked up **(figure 2)**. (Note: You are using all lower holes of the QuadraTile.)

4. Pick up a Bar and two 11ºs, sew through the last 11º added in the previous step, and continue through the next two Bars, the three 11ºs, and the next Bar. Continue through the first bead picked up at the start of this step **(figures 3 and 4)**.

5. Pick up an 11º, a 3mm, an 11º, a QuadraTile, a Tile, a QuadraTile, an 11º, a 3mm, two 11ºs, and a Bar, and sew through the available hole in the Bar at the end of this row **(figure 5)**. The first unit is not complete at this point; you will do that at the end. Pull snug.

FIGURE 1

FIGURE 2

FIGURE 4

FIGURE 3

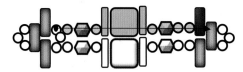

FIGURE 5

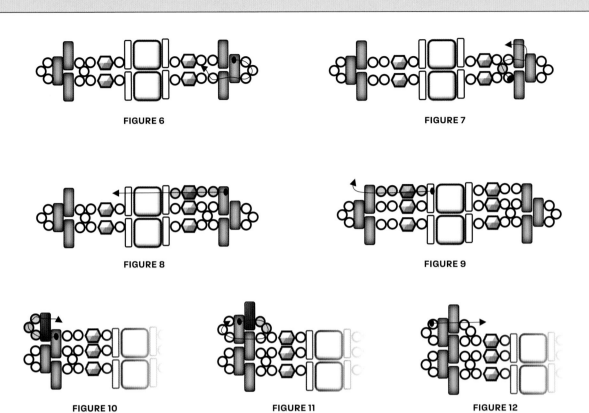

FIGURE 6

FIGURE 7

FIGURE 8

FIGURE 9

FIGURE 10

FIGURE 11

FIGURE 12

6. Continue through the three edge picot 11°s and two Bars, and the following 11° (**figure 6**). Pick up an 11°, and make a turn by sewing through the 11° closest to the adjoining Bar and first Bar to connect the two strips of beads. Turn and sew through the available hole in the Bar your thread is exiting (**figure 7**).

hint **If your tension needs to be tighter, try spinning around the Bar and 11° picot before turning on the Bar.**

7. Pick up two 11°s, a 3mm, and an 11°, and sew through the corresponding holes of the next QuadraTile, Tile, and QuadraTile (**figure 8**). Pick up an 11°, a 3mm, and two 11°s, and sew through the available hole of the next Bar (**figure 9**).

8. Pick up a Bar and three 11°s, and make the turn by sewing back through the available hole of the Bar your thread is exiting (**figure 10**).

9. Work as in step 4 (**figures 11 and 12**).

10. Work as in step 5 (**figure 13**).

11. Pick up an 11°, and sew through the 11° closest to the adjoining Bar and first Bar. Repeat steps 7–11 to the desired length, ending with step 7 and ending and adding thread as needed. On the final unit, complete the hint at step 6 to secure.

12. Close the gap at both ends with a fill-in, as in step 7. Sew back through the final Bar, pick up a 15° seed bead (**figure 14**), and sew back through the same hole of the Bar. The 15° acts as a "catch bead." Reinforce the thread path through the connecting beads, and use a 15° as a catch bead on the other end of the row.

13. Sew through the next 11° with the needle pointing toward the opposite edge. Pick up an 11°, a 4mm, and an 11°, and sew through the upper hole of the next QuadraTile. On the very first unit only, turn to the lower level of the bracelet, and then use the Tile to sew to the next QuadraTile. Sew from the Tile to exit the upper hole of the QuadraTile, and pick up an 11°, a 4mm, and an 11°, and sew through the last 11° and Bar in this row. Make the turn by sewing through the second hole of the Bar and the next 11° (**figure 15**). You are now ready to start the repeating pattern.

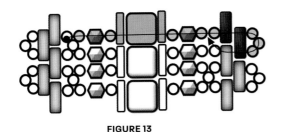

FIGURE 13

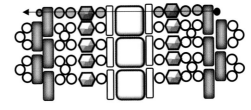

FIGURE 14

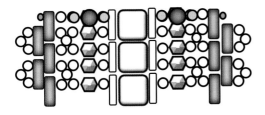

FIGURE 15

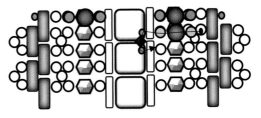

FIGURE 16

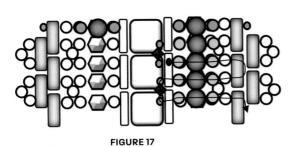

FIGURE 17

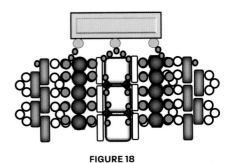

FIGURE 18

14. Pick up an 11º, a 4mm, and an 11º, and sew through the next open hole of the QuadraTile. Pick up a 15º, a 3mm crystal, and a 15º, and sew through the next open hole of the next QuadraTile, reversing direction **(figure 16)**. Pick up an 11º, a 4mm, and an 11º, and sew through the next 11º and Bar. Sew through the second hole of the Bar, and the next 11º. Repeat, working one side only for the entire length **(figure 17)**. Then, sew through the beadwork and repeat this pattern on the other side of the bracelet to match.

15. Attach the clasp by exiting a side 3mm and picking up two or three 15ºs or 11ºs and the nearest loop of one half of the clasp **(figure 18)**. Reinforce the connection several times. (The center loop of the clasp is connected to the beads on either side of the center QuadraTile, Tile, QuadraTile set). Repeat to attach the remaining loops of the clasp, and end the working thread. Repeat this step using the tail to attach the other half of the clasp to the opposite end of the bracelet.

Marcia's Tip

Use a permanent marker to color your thread when color really matters. Use crystal Fireline, and just dab the marker on the thread where it shows—or color the whole thread by putting down a piece of scrap paper and pulling the Fireline along under the fat tip of the marker.

all wrapped up bracelet

This is a variation of a common design using three-hole Trinity beads as part of the center. The Trinity beads give real depth to the piece.

Supplies

- **18–25** 8x8mm Trinity beads
- **34–48** 6mm round beads
- **34–48** 4mm fire-polished beads
- **34–48** 3mm bicone crystals
- **34–48** 2mm fire-polished beads
- 7g SuperDuo beads
- 5g O-beads
- 5g 11º seed beads in each of **2** colors: A, B
- 5g 15º seed beads
- One- or two-hole clasp
- Scissors
- Beading needles, size 11 or 12
- Fireline, 8-lb. test, or thread of your choice

MAKE THE BRACELET

1. Thread a needle on a comfortable length of thread, and use a Trinity bead as a stop bead to secure your thread by sewing through a base hole, leaving an 8-in. (20cm) tail. Pick up a repeating pattern of a 6mm round bead and the base hole of a Trinity to the desired length

(figure 1). You must sew through the corresponding base hole of each Trinity so the point hole is either facing you or facing your work surface. The base holes will be along the back of your work, and the point holes will be used to secure the embellishment along the top of the bracelet. This piece will shrink about ½ in. (1.3cm), so keep that in mind as you choose the length. The center hole of the Trinity is not yet illustrated **(figure 2)**.

2. Add a second row of 6mms between the available base holes of the Trinitys **(figure 3)**.

3. At the end of the second row, turn and sew through the first base hole of the end Trinity, and continue through the adjacent 6mm and the corresponding base hold in the next Trinity **(figure 4)**.

4. Add your first wing pattern: Pick up a 15º seed bead, a color A 11º seed bead, a color B 11º seed bead, an O-bead, a SuperDuo, a 4mm fire-polished bead, a

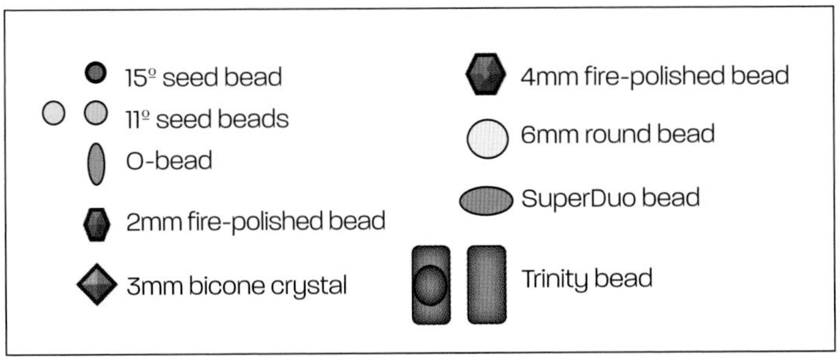

Legend

- 15º seed bead
- 11º seed beads
- O-bead
- 2mm fire-polished bead
- 3mm bicone crystal
- 4mm fire-polished bead
- 6mm round bead
- SuperDuo bead
- Trinity bead

FIGURE 1

FIGURE 2

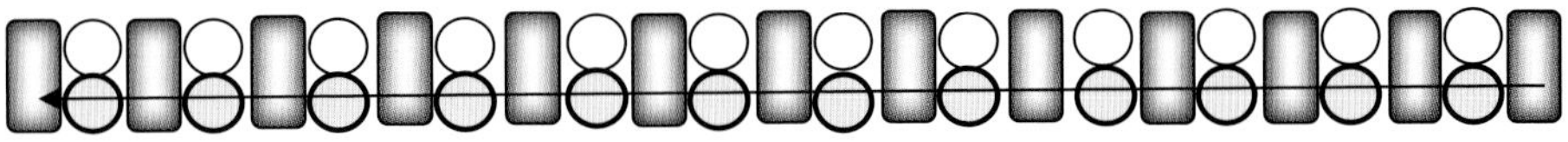

FIGURE 3

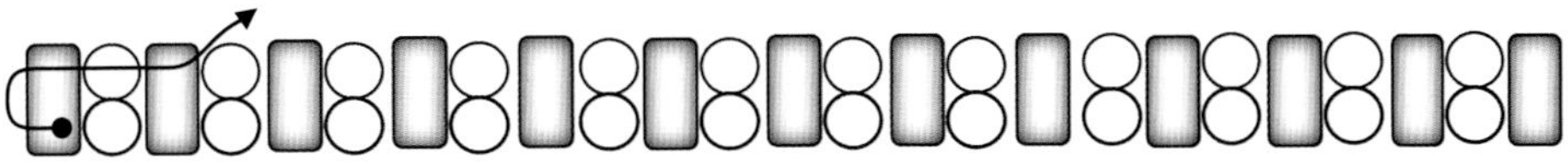

FIGURE 4

FIGURE 5

FIGURE 6

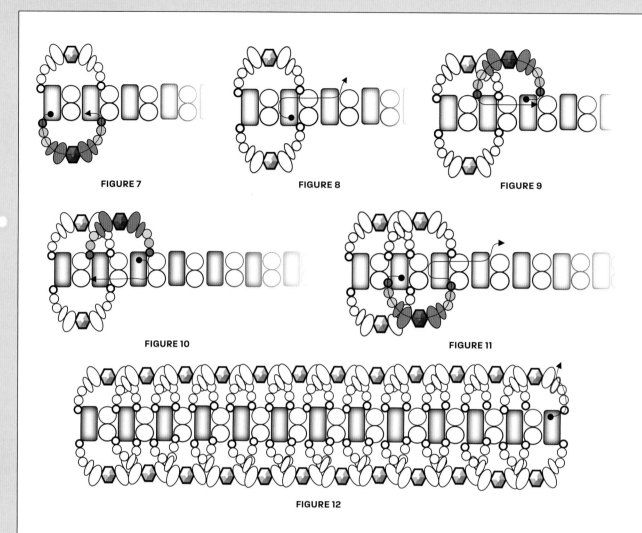

FIGURE 7

FIGURE 8

FIGURE 9

FIGURE 10

FIGURE 11

FIGURE 12

SuperDuo, an O-bead, a B, an A, and a 15º, and sew back through the same hole of the end Trinity, the 6mm and the next Trinity. Your thread will be exiting the same location as at the start of this step **(figure 5)**.

5. Turn and sew through the other base hole of the same Trinity, the adjacent 6mm, and the corresponding hole of the end Trinity **(figure 6)**.

6. Pick up a 15º, an A, a B, an O-bead, a SuperDuo, a 4mm, a SuperDuo, an O-bead, a B, an A, and a 15º, and sew through the corresponding base hole of the second Trinity with the needle pointing toward the end of the band to create the wing pattern on this side of the bracelet **(figure 7)**.

7. Turn and sew through the other base hole of the same Trinity, and continue through the adjacent 6mm and base hole of the following Trinity **(figure 8)**.

8. Pick up the wing pattern from step 4 (each new wing will slightly overlap the previous wing and be positioned on top of the wing before it). Sew through the corresponding base hole of the previous Trinity bead, and continue through the 6mm and the Trinity bead your thread exited at the start of this step, with the needle pointing away from the tail **(figure 9)**. Watch your thread as you sew the wing pattern on to the top. It is easy to get on the wrong side. Double-check to make sure your second wing is on top of the previous one.

9. Make a turn as in step 5 **(figure 10)**.

10. Work as in step 6 **(figure 11)**.

11. Continue adding wings, repeating steps 7–10 for the length of the bracelet, ending and adding thread as needed. Be careful to add beads on the same side each time you add new wings. It is critical to maintain the

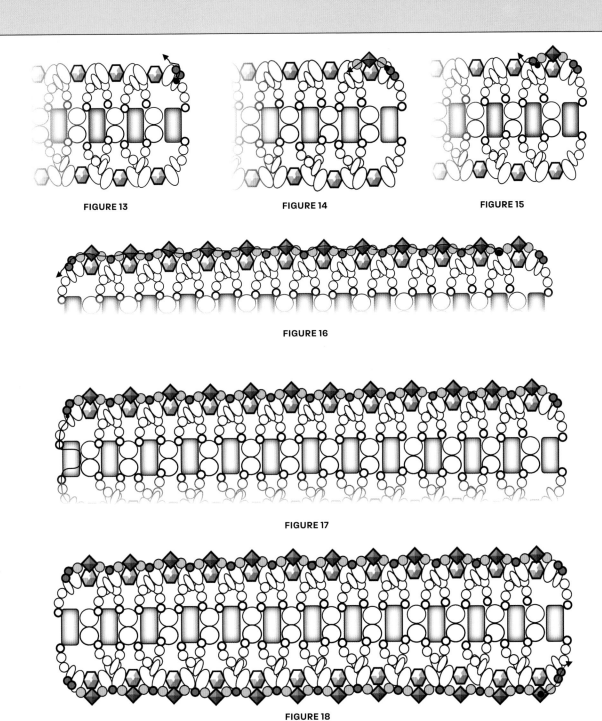

FIGURE 13

FIGURE 14

FIGURE 15

FIGURE 16

FIGURE 17

FIGURE 18

pattern. At the end of the band, sew through the beads in a wing to exit the nearest O-bead with your needle pointing toward the opposite end (highlighted red) (**figure 12**).

12. Pick up two 15°s, and sew through the available hole of the nearest SuperDuo (**figure 13**).

13. Pick up an 11°, a 3mm bicone, and an 11°, and sew through the available hole of the next SuperDuo (**figure 14**).

14. Pick up a 15°, and sew through the available hole of the next SuperDuo (**figure 15**). It will be tight.

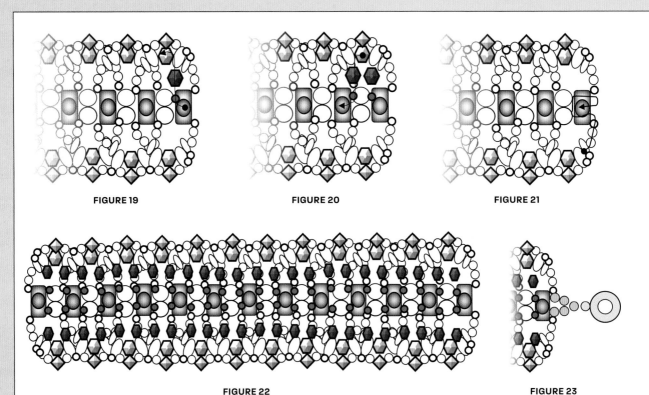

FIGURE 19

FIGURE 20

FIGURE 21

FIGURE 22

FIGURE 23

15. Repeat steps 13 and 14 to the end of the bracelet. At the very last connection, pick up two 15ºs, and sew through the next O-bead on this end of the bracelet **(figure 16)**.

16. Sew through the beadwork to exit the corresponding O-bead along the other edge of the bracelet. Repeat steps 12–15 **(figures 17 and 18)**.

17. Sew through the beadwork to exit the point hole of the first Trinity. (Note the center hole of the Trinity is now illustrated.)

18. Pick up a 15º and a 2mm fire-polished bead (or 11º, if desired), and sew through the next 4mm **(figure 19)**. Pick up a 2mm and a 15º, and sew through the next point hole of the Trinity. Pull slightly to fold the outer wings up to the top **(figure 20)**.

19. Repeat step 18 to the end of the bracelet **(figure 21)**. Repeat on the other side of the bracelet **(figure 22)**.

20. Connect a clasp using the two lower holes of the Trinity and a few seed beads **(figure 23)**. Exit the end Trinity. Pick up three 11ºs and one half of the clasp, and pass back through the closest seed bead to the clasp.

Marcia's Tip

"Stop and admire your work." This is actually Marilyn Earhart's phrase. I used to say, "Watch what you are doing," but this is a much nicer way to ask to you pay attention.

The goal is to catch a thread that is in the wrong place before it is difficult or too late to fix. Mistakes happen: You'll pull your needle and thread or bead through your beadwork quickly and continue to bead. Then you'll look back and discover you snagged your working thread on the beadwork and have a thread showing. Or maybe you quickly sewed into the wrong bead. It is easy to fix if it is caught right away. The bottom line is: Pay attention!

Pick up two more 11ºs, and pass through the other hole of the Trinity. Reinforce. (To attach a two-part clasp, repeat for the second loop of the clasp.) Repeat on the other end of the bracelet.

stargazer pendant

This stunning piece is made of three-hole Trinity beads with seed beads, crystals, pearls, and a cabochon. Add beaded strap of your choice for a simple, yet elegant design.

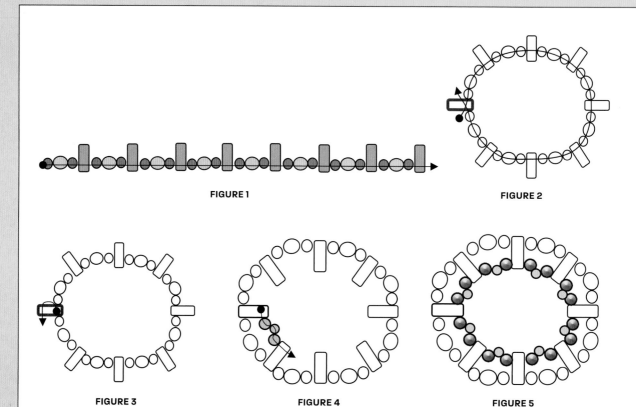

FIGURE 1

FIGURE 2

FIGURE 3

FIGURE 4

FIGURE 5

Intermediate

Supplies

- **5** (1 per pendant) 18mm cabochon
- 10x12mm drop or bead of choice
- **80** (**16** per pendant) 4mm bicone crystals
- **40** (**8** per pendant) 4mm fire-polish beads
- **120** (**24** per pendant) 3mm pearls
- **120** (**24** per pendant) 2mm fire-polished beads
- **80** (**16** per pendant) Trinity beads
- 2g 8º seed beads
- 7g 11º seed beads in **4** colors: A, B, C, D
- 2g 15º seed beads
- One- or two-hole clasp
- Scissors
- Beading needles, size 11 or 12
- Fireline, 6-lb. test, or thread of your choice

NOTE: Adding a drop and connection to the pendant will require more beads. A Trinity bead is a triangle-shaped bead with three holes. For the purposes of these project instructions, position the Trinity beads so two holes sit side-by-side at the base of the triangle, and a single hole is at the point of the triangle. The holes will be identified as base holes and a point hole so you know which hole to sew through as the bead is positioned in the project.

MAKE THE PENDANT

1. Thread a needle on 2 yd. (1.8m) of thread.

2. Work in a circular pattern to create the piece. Pick up a repeating pattern of a color A 11º seed bead, a 3mm pearl, an A, and the base hole of a Trinity bead eight times for a total of 32 beads **(figure 1)**. Sew through all the beads again to form a ring, leaving an 8-in. (20cm) tail **(figure 2)**. Tie an overhand knot with the working thread and the tail, and then sew through all the beads again. Turn, and sew through the available base hole of the Trinity **(figure 3)**.

3. Pick up a 2mm fire-polished bead, a color D 11º seed bead, and a 2mm, and sew through the available base hole of the next Trinity **(figure 4)**. Repeat to finish the round **(figure 5)**.

4. Turn and sew through the point hole of a Trinity. Pick up 3mm, a Trinity, and a 3mm, and sew through the point hole of the next Trinity **(figure 6)**. Repeat to finish the round **(figure 7)**. Retrace the thread path through all the beads in this step to reinforce. Step up through the first 3mm and Trinity picked up.

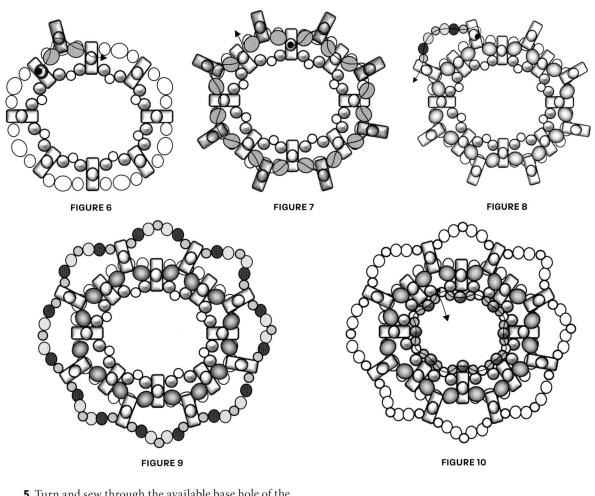

FIGURE 6

FIGURE 7

FIGURE 8

FIGURE 9

FIGURE 10

5. Turn and sew through the available base hole of the same Trinity your thread exited at the start of this step. You are working on the back of the piece. (The front has the 2mms.) Pick up a 15º seed bead, an A, a color B 11º seed bead, a 15º, a B, an A, and a 15º, and sew through the available base hole of the next Trinity **(figure 8)**. Repeat to finish the round **(figure 9)**.

6. With the tail, sew through the beadwork to the front inside edge to exit an 11º. Pick up a 15º, a 2mm, and a 15º, and sew through the next 11º. Repeat to complete the round and retrace the thread path through the beads in this step to reinforce **(figure 10)**. End the tail. The cabochon should fit at this point, but don't place it just yet.

7. With the working thread, sew through the beadwork to exit the center 15º picked up in step 5. Pick up an A, a B, a 15º, a B, and an A, and sew through the next center 15º **(figure 11)**. Repeat this stitch three times, and

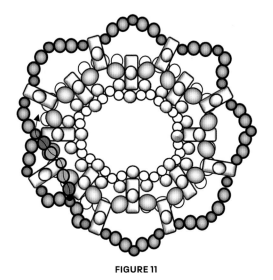

FIGURE 11

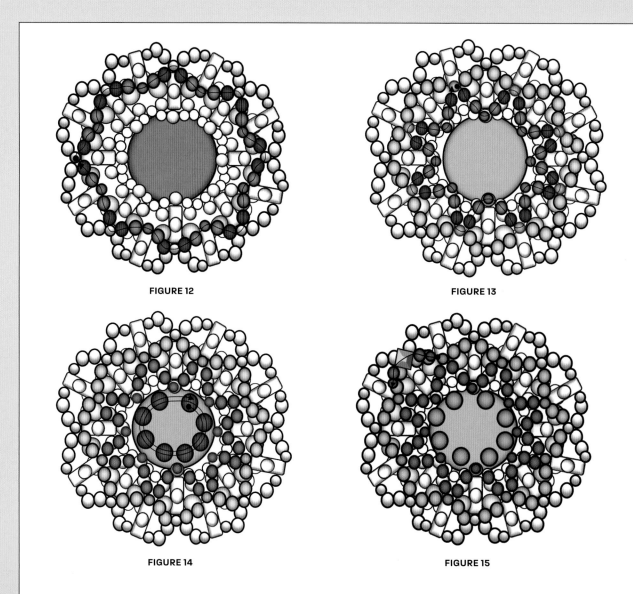

FIGURE 12

FIGURE 13

FIGURE 14

FIGURE 15

then place the cabochon in the beadwork so the back of the cabochon rests on the beads in step 6, and then complete the round **(figure 12)**. Step up through the first three beads added in this step.

8. Pick up an A, a B, a 15º, a B, and an A, and sew through the next 15º picked up in the previous round (highlighted red) **(figure 13)**. Repeat to complete the round, and step up through the first three beads picked up in this round to exit a 15º.

9. Pick up an 8º seed bead, and sew through the next 15º picked up in the previous round (highlighted red) **(figure 14)**. Repeat to complete the round, and then sew through only the 8ºs in this round again, using a firm tension to secure the cabochon in the beadwork.

10. Sew through the beadwork to exit the inner base hole of a Trinity picked up in step 4; you are working on the back of the piece and will use this hole a second time. Pick up a 15º, an A, a 4mm crystal, an A, and a 15º, and sew through the base hole of the corresponding Trinity **(figure 15)**. Work the round. You are working on the back **(figure 16)**.

11. Sew through the beadwork to exit the other base hole of the Trinity along the outer-most edge of the piece. Pick up an 8º, a color C 11º, a 4mm fire-polished bead, a C, and an 8º, and sew through the next Trinity around the circle **(figure 17)**. Repeat all around and reinforce this round. You are now working on the front.

12. Sew through the beadwork to exit a fire-polished

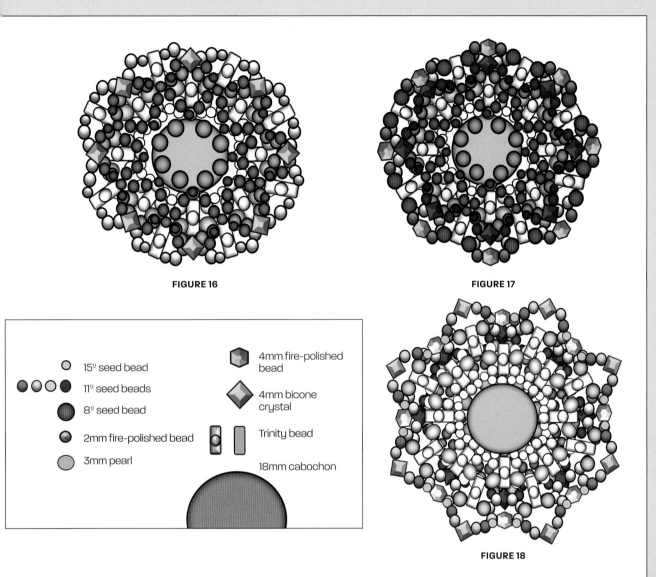

FIGURE 16

FIGURE 17

15º seed bead

11º seed beads

8º seed bead

2mm fire-polished bead

3mm pearl

4mm fire-polished bead

4mm bicone crystal

Trinity bead

18mm cabochon

FIGURE 18

bead on the outer circle. Pick up a 15º, a C, a color D 11º, a 4mm crystal, a D, a C, and a 15º, and sew through the next fire-polished bead **(figure 18)**. Repeat around the circle, and reinforce.

MAKE A MULTI-FOCAL NECKLACE

13. Repeat steps 1–12 to make as many components as you like (I made five). The components may be connected at various points, depending on your choice of number of components and style desired. Exit a crystal from one component to join to the next. Notice in the picture how the number of beads between the center and next focal will change on upper and lower components to get the desired fit. Add a drop bead, if desired, in the middle of a loop of beads of your choice exiting the center lowest fire-polished bead.

Marcia's Tip

Pop out a wrong bead—don't crush it! Sometimes you'll notice an extra bead in your work and want to remove it by destroying it. I use a Tulip Awl to pop it out rather than pliers to crush it in toward the thread. When you crush a bead with pliers, the glass you are smashing could cut or weaken the thread. When you pop it out by exploding the bead with an awl, you are shattering the glass out with almost no chance that you will cut your thread.

advanced

eye of the tiger bracelet

Watch the Crescent and Trinity beads as you make this piece. When you pick up the beads correctly, the symmetry of the piece simply sings!

Supplies

- **34–48** 6mm fire-polished beads
- **34–48** 4mm fire-polished beads
- **34–48** 3mm fire-polished beads
- **18–25** Trinity beads
- 7g Crescent beads
- 5g 8° demi round seed beads
- 5g 11° seed beads, plus a few grams in a contrasting color
- 5g 15° seed beads
- Two-hole clasp
- Scissors
- Beading needles, size 11 or 12
- Fireline, 6-lb. test, or thread of your choice

MAKE THE BRACELET

1. You will start by building the base the full length. Choose a clasp at the start to judge the length needed. Thread a needle on a comfortable length of thread, and secure the thread using two holes of a Trinity bead as a stop bead **(figure 1)**. You may start at the midpoint with half of the thread on a spool (see "Marcia's Tip," p. 46).

2. Pick up a 6mm fire-polished bead, a Trinity, a 6mm, and a Trinity, and repeat the pattern to the desired length. Finish with a Trinity **(figure 2)**. This piece will shrink about ½ in. (1.3cm), so take that into consideration.

3. Sew through an adjacent hole of the Trinity, and then add a second row of 6mms between the Trinitys using these holes **(figure 3)**. These holes will become the base holes. Pay attention to the point hole of the Trinity; you must have them all pointing the same way.

4. Turn, and sew back through the first base hole of the Trinity and continue through the next three beads picked up in step 2 to exit the second 6mm **(figure 4)**.

FIGURE 1   FIGURE 2

FIGURE 3

FIGURE 4

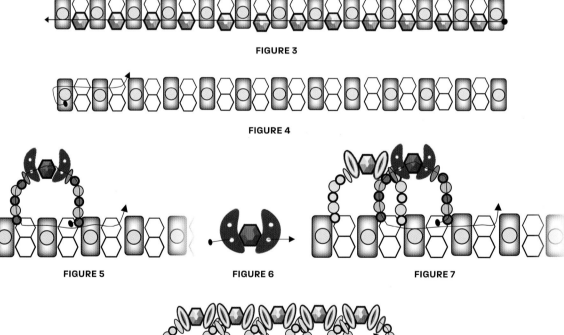

FIGURE 5   FIGURE 6   FIGURE 7

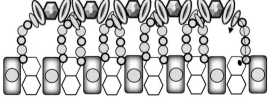

FIGURE 8

5. Add the first wing pattern: Pick up a 15º seed bead, an 11º seed bead, a 15º, an 11º, a 15º, an 8º demi-round seed bead, a Crescent bead, a 4mm fire-polished bead, a Crescent, an 8º, a 15º, an 11º, a 15º, an 11º, and a 15º. Sew back through the previous 6mm, Trinity, 6mm, Trinity, and 6mm in the same direction **(figure 5)**. Be sure to pick up the Crescents properly; the points should be poking up at this stage, "smiling" **(figure 6)**. They will flip over to the center later.

6. Repeat the wing pattern to the end of the row **(figure 7)**, each new wing will slightly overlap and lay on top of the previous wing.

7. Sew through a wing pattern to exit the first 8º (highlighted red) **(figure 8)**.

8. Pick up three 15ºs, and sew through the available hole of the Crescent **(figure 9)**. (Note this bead will now be flipped to the inside.)

9. Pick up an 11º, a 3mm, and an 11º, and sew through the available hole of the next Crescent **(figure 10)**.

10. Pick up an 8º, and sew through the available hole of the next Crescent **(figure 11)**. Flip and pull tight.

11. Repeat steps 9 and 10 to the end, ending and adding thread as needed. At the last connection, pick up three 15ºs, and sew through the 8º (highlighted red) **(figure 12)**.

12. The final connection to the center uses an 11º before and after the 3mm between the upper holes of the Trinitys (highlighted red). Turn and retrace the thread path to exit the 11º before the 3mm. Use the 15º to turn around and retrace **(figure 13)**.

13. From the 11º after the Crescent, pick up an 11º in a contrasting color and a 15º, and sew through the point hole of the Trinity **(figure 14)**. Pick up a 15º and an 11º, and sew through the next 11º and continue through the Crescent, 8º, Crescent, and 11º. Continue connecting from the 11º on either side of the 3mm to the point hole of the corresponding Trinity with the combination of the 15º and 11º, alternating the pickup order.

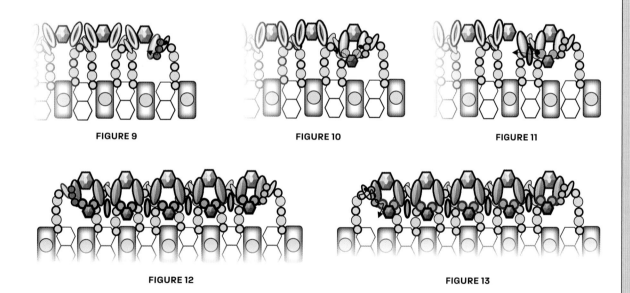

FIGURE 9   **FIGURE 10**   **FIGURE 11**

FIGURE 12   **FIGURE 13**

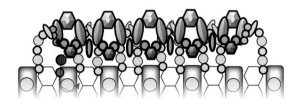

FIGURE 14

14. Repeat step 13 to the end (figure 15).

15. Exit the last Crescent. Pick up an 11º, a 3mm, and an 11º, and sew through the point hole of the last Trinity. You are finished with one side (figure 16).

16. Repeat steps 4–14 on the other side from the same starting point as the first side.

17. At the end of the second side, complete the last connection to the Trinity. Exit the last Crescent. Pick up an 11º and a 3mm, and sew through the shared 11º and Trinity. The 11º is shared by the two sides to center the final connection (highlighted). This closes the gap on both ends. Finish the open end with the tail or a new thread (figure 17).

18. To attach the clasp: Sew through the beadwork to exit a base hole of an end Trinity, pick up one or two 11ºs, and sew through a loop on one half of the two-loop clasp. Sew back through the 11º and the same hole of the Trinity. Turn and sew through the remaining base hole of the Trinity, pick up an 11º and the available loop of the clasp. Sew back through the 11º and the Trinity (figure 18). Retrace the thread path through both connections to the clasp to secure and end the working thread. Repeat this step using the tail and the other half of the clasp for the other end of the bracelet. End the thread.

Marcia's Tip

You will inevitably need to add thread. For years, I took a long piece of thread to avoid adding. I now know, having learned the hard way, that you are better off with a shorter length of thread. Now, I usually take just over a wing span or about 4 ft. (1.22m) for most projects.

Shorter threads mean that you will avoid knots and sew faster. It takes time, when you must pull and pull to work your long thread through the beadwork. It will get tangled more and knot more. Pulling lots of thread through the beadwork will also weaken the thread, particularly if you are working with crystals or pressed glass beads.

I have also learned not to almost double the thread and "move it along" as you work. Two things will happen when you do this: First, the eye of the needle is creating a tiny weakness in the thread. Second, the long tail will wrap along the working thread, increasing your chances for getting tangled and knotted.

There are times when you can take double the amount of thread that you are comfortable with and "park" the thread; see "Marcia's Tip," p. 46.

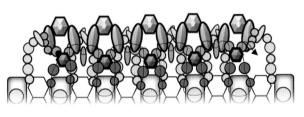

FIGURE 15

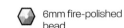

15º seed bead	6mm fire-polished bead
11º seed beads	
8º demi-round bead	Trinity bead
3mm fire-polished bead	
4mm fire-polished bead	Crescent bead

FIGURE 16   **FIGURE 17**   **FIGURE 18**

irish tweed bracelet

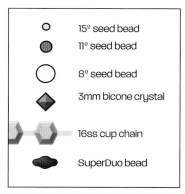

This lesson assumes you already know basic odd-count peyote. Odd-count peyote is a little harder, but for any centered design of color or embellishment, it is necessary.

Supplies

- **40** 3mm bicone crystals
- 7g SuperDuo beads
- 15g 8º seed beads
- 5g 11º seed beads
- 5g 15º seed beads
- 7–9 in. (18–23cm) cup chain, 16ss (4mm)
- Two- or three-hole clasp
- Scissors
- Beading needles, size 11 or 12
- Fireline, 6-lb. test, or thread of your choice

FIGURE 1

MAKE THE BRACELET

1. Start with the longest piece of thread you are comfortable using. I used 3 yd. (2.7m) to start my bracelet base for about 6¾ in. (17.1cm). (You may not want to use that much, and it is very easy to add thread in peyote with 8º seed beads.) Place a bead stopper at the middle of the thread. Pick up a wrist-length amount of beads in an **odd** number (mine has 83) **(figure 1)**.

Sizing note: Measuring from the initial string of beads will result in a bracelet that is too long. After you start to work peyote, the beads will spread out a little. You generally need to start with a length at least 1 in. (2.5cm) shorter than your wrist. Then, when you work peyote back the first time, do a double-check at the end of the row before turning to make sure the length is correct (minus the clasp). It is easy to adjust at this point. Refer to "Truly Embellished," p. 29, steps 2–4 for basic odd-count peyote directions and illustrations.

2. To fit the cup chain, cut an extra ½ in. (1.3cm) or so. You will need more than the length of your bracelet

○	15º seed bead
◉	11º seed bead
○	8º seed bead
◆	3mm bicone crystal
⬡⬡	16ss cup chain
⬮	SuperDuo bead

blank lying flat, as it will take up more space to curve. Center your cup chain to stitch over each length of metal. You will be stitching out of different beads as you stitch down, as the cup chain does not match the base. I rolled the base over a couple of my finger to get the fit right. Don't sew it flat; it needs to curve slightly to work. It will work best if you watch the spacing with each stitch and move it from flat to curved to see which beads will work best.

3. Exit a bead on one side of the chain, pick up five 15º seed beads, and pass through the bead on the other side, heading backwards (**figure 2**). Travel under the cup on the diagonal to the next blank space (**figure 3**). You will be passing through two or three beads under the cup chain from a seven-bead-wide row to a six-bead-wide row, and back and forth. Stretch and flatten, and study which beads will fit best (**figures 4–7**).

hint **If you are not a precision beader, you can cheat. Instead of all the backtracking, sew forward on the diagonal to add the 15ºs. It will work with an ever-so-slightly different look, as the beads will be on a slight angle not perfectly straight over the cup chain. This method is faster, if less precise.**

4. Add the SuperDuos: Exit an 8º in a seven-bead-wide row heading away from the length of the bracelet (**figure 8**). (The first four beads used to sew the SuperDuo unit onto the bracelet are highlighted red.) Note the Super-Duo units do not align with the cup chain. This whole 8º-and-SuperDuo unit is not sewn in a straight line. (It could be, as it would be easier—but it wouldn't look as nice!) Pick up a 15º, an 11º, a 15º, a SuperDuo, a 15º, an 11º, and a 15º, and pass back through the next 8º in line, heading away from the length again. Travel on the diagonal over to the edge 8º. Pick up a 15º, an 11º, and a 15º, and pass through the open hole of the SuperDuo. Pick up a 15º, an 11º, and a 15º again, and pass back through the next 8º in line. Travel again under the SuperDuo topper on the diagonal to the next 8º next to the cup chain. Repeat to the end of the bracelet (**figures 9–13**).

5. Fill the ditch along the side with 11ºs (**figures 14 and 15**).

6. To make a side picot, exit an end 11º used to fill the ditch. Pick up a 15º, an 11º, a 3mm crystal, an 11º, and a 15º, skip an 11º edge bead, and pass through the next 11º. Repeat to the end (**figure 16**). Sew through the beadwork to exit an 11º on the other edge, and repeat.

7. Reinforce the entire edge by sewing through each picot to picot, passing through the 11º edge bead as well.

8. Add a clasp by sewing through the beadwork, picking up a bead, a loop of the clasp, and a bead, and sewing through the bracelet (**figure 17**). Reinforce.

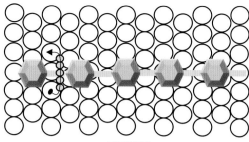

FIGURE 2

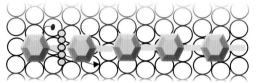

FIGURE 3

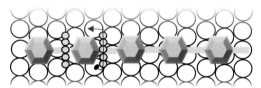

FIGURE 4

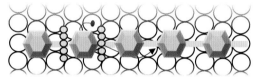

FIGURE 5

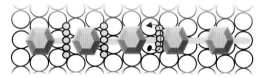

FIGURE 6

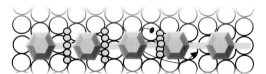

FIGURE 7

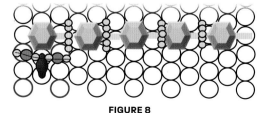

FIGURE 8

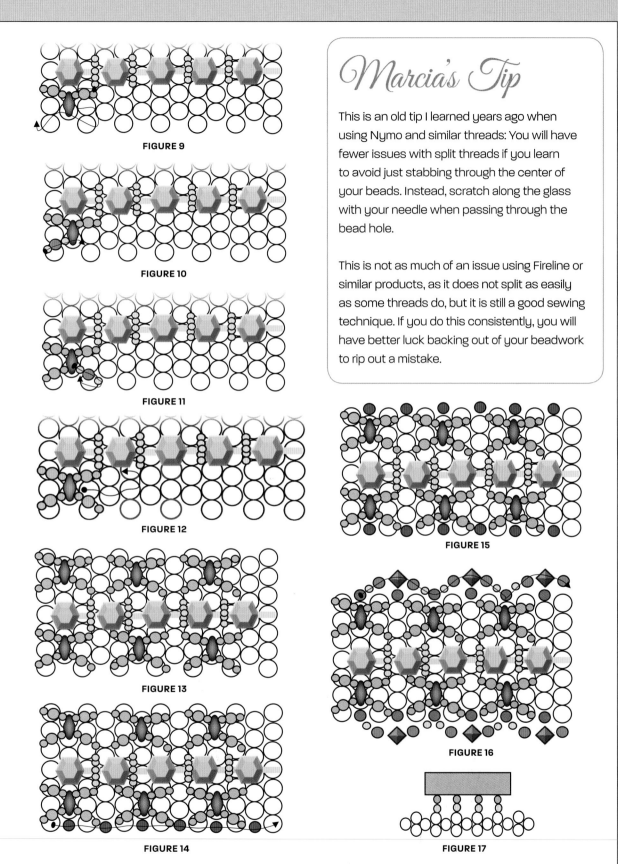

FIGURE 9

FIGURE 10

FIGURE 11

FIGURE 12

FIGURE 13

FIGURE 14

Marcia's Tip

This is an old tip I learned years ago when using Nymo and similar threads: You will have fewer issues with split threads if you learn to avoid just stabbing through the center of your beads. Instead, scratch along the glass with your needle when passing through the bead hole.

This is not as much of an issue using Fireline or similar products, as it does not split as easily as some threads do, but it is still a good sewing technique. If you do this consistently, you will have better luck backing out of your beadwork to rip out a mistake.

FIGURE 15

FIGURE 16

FIGURE 17

beam-me-up bracelet

This variation of a flat spiral design uses three-hole Beam beads as part of the foundation and center. It is also not suitable as a clasped bracelet for wrists 6 in. (15cm) and under. You could easily make this as a bangle, too!

Supplies

- **48–62** 4mm fire-polished or round beads
- **12–15** 4mm fire-polished beads in a contrasting color
- **48–52** 3mm fire-polished, melon, or English-cut beads
- **49–56** three-hole Beam beads
- **24–28** 3x5mm Pinch beads
- 7g mini SuperDuos
- 5g 8º demi round seed beads
- 5g 11º seed beads
- 5g 15º seed beads
- Two-hole clasp
- Scissors
- Beading needles, size 11 or 12
- Fireline, 6-lb. test, or thread of your choice

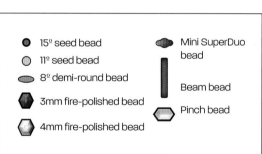

● 15º seed bead	Mini SuperDuo bead
○ 11º seed bead	
◯ 8º demi-round bead	Beam bead
⬡ 3mm fire-polished bead	
⬡ 4mm fire-polished bead	⬡ Pinch bead

MAKE THE BRACELET

1. This piece starts with the core base the full desired length. Thread a needle on a comfortable length of thread, and sew through two holes of the Beam bead to secure your thread. leaving a 6-in. (15cm) tail. Next, pick up a repeating pattern of a 4mm fire-polished bead and an outer hole of a Beam to the desired length, ending with a Beam (you must use an even number of 4mms) **(figure 1)**. This piece will tighten a little as you build up the height.

hint **End with a 4mm to join to the first Beam. You must use an even number of 4mms for the bangle. Reinforce. My bangle has 30 4mms on each side.**

2. Turn, and sew through the middle hole of the Beam your thread is exiting. Pick up a 15º seed bead, and sew back through the same hole of the Beam again. Then turn, and sew through the remaining available outer hole of the Beam. Add a second row of 4mms between the Beams, using the available outer hole of each Beam **(figure 2)**.

FIGURE 1

FIGURE 2

FIGURE 3

FIGURE 4

hint **Turn using the Beam. You will be working around in different directions. Reinforce.**

3. At the end of the band, turn and sew through the middle hole of the Beam, and add the center connection from Beam to Beam by picking up a 15º, sewing through the middle hole of another Beam, and picking up a 15º **(figure 3)**. End by sewing through the 15º added in step 2 and the middle hole of the end Beam. Sew through the beadwork to exit the second 4mm on one side **(figure 4)**. This Beam added is standing up.

4. Add the first wing pattern: Working toward the tail, pick up a 15º, an 11º seed bead, a Mini SuperDuo bead, an 8º demi round seed bead, a 3mm fire-polished bead, an 8º, a Mini SuperDuo, an 11º, and a 15º, and sew back through the previous 4mm, the adjacent hole in the next B **(figure 5)**, the 4mm your thread exited at the start of this step, and the following Beam and 4mm to be in position to create the next wing **(figure 6)**. Repeat this step for the length of the bracelet **(figure 7)**, ending and adding thread as needed.

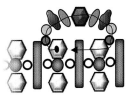

FIGURE 5

FIGURE 6

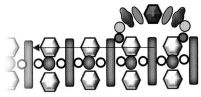

FIGURE 7

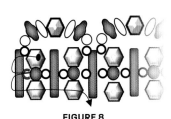

FIGURE 8

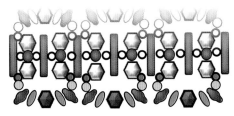

FIGURE 9

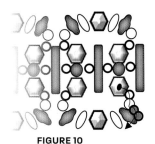

FIGURE 10

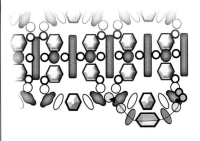

FIGURE 11

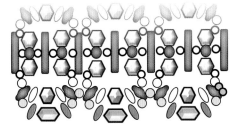

FIGURE 12

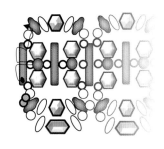

FIGURE 13

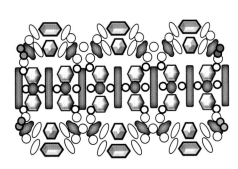

FIGURE 14

FIGURE 15

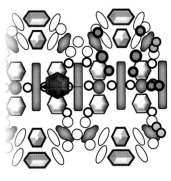

FIGURE 16

5. To make the turn and be in position to add the wings to the other edge, sew through the middle hole of the end Beam and the following 11º with the needle pointing toward the opposite end. Skip the 11º, and sew back through the middle hole in the Beam. Turn and sew through the adjacent outer hole of the Beam, the 4mm, Beam, and 4mm along this edge **(figure 8)**. Repeat the wing pattern along this edge **(figure 9)**.

6. Sew through the last wing to exit the 11º before the Mini SuperDuo to begin the next connection. Pick up two 15ºs, and sew through the available hole of the Mini SuperDuo **(figure 10)**. These two-bead pickups will be required at several steps.

7. Pick up an 11º, an 8º, a Pinch bead, an 8º, and an 11º, and sew through the available hole of the next Mini SuperDuo **(figure 11)**. The difference in bead choices depends on seed beads used and tension. Fit the space so when you pull tight, no thread shows. Continue picking up the alternating pattern of beads to the end **(figure 12)**.

8. At the end of the row, and with your thread exiting the available hole of the last wing, pick up two 15ºs, and sew through the 11º and 15º in the wing and the nearest hole in the end Beam. Turn, and sew through the middle hole of the end Beam and the following 11º with the needle pointing toward the opposite end. Skip

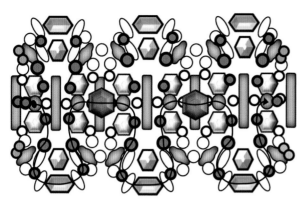

FIGURE 17

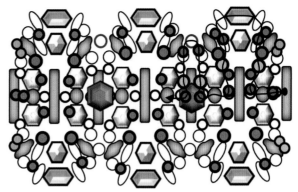

FIGURE 18

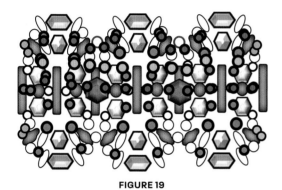

FIGURE 19

FIGURE 20

the 11º, and sew back through the middle hole in the Beam, turn, and sew through the adjacent outer hole of the Beam and the 15º and 11º **(figure 13)**. Complete this edge as in steps 6 and 7. Pick up two 15ºs at the end of the row **(figure 14)**.

9. Sew through the middle hole of the base Beam. Sew up to the standing-up Beam and add a middle connection by picking up two 15ºs. Exit the middle hole of the protruding Beam.

10. Pick up a 15º, an 11º, and a 15º, and sew through the 8º, Pinch bead, and 8º added in step 7. This will pull the wing into the center. Pick up a 15º, an 11º, and a 15º, and sew through the center hole of the next protruding Beam **(figure 15)**.

11. Pick up a 4mm in a bright contrasting color (you will only see a hint of this bead when done). Sew through the middle hole of the next Beam **(figure 16)**.

12. Repeat steps 10 and 11 to the end of the bracelet. Exit the last protruding Beam with a 15º. Exit the Beam edge. Pick up a 15º, and pass back through the same hole of the Beam.

13. Repeat step 10 on the other edge of the bracelet, sewing through the center 4mm between the Beams added in step 12 **(figure 17)**.

14. Sew through the beadwork to the upper hole of the center Beam with a 15º. Pick up a 15º, an 11º, and a 15º (you can also substitute other beads; try three 15ºs, for example). Sew through an 8º, a Pinch, and an 8º **(figure 18)**. These beads are laying on top of the same beads from step 11. Pick up a 15º, an 11º, and a 15º, and sew through the next Beam. Pick up a 15º, an 11º, and a 15º, and sew through the 11º added between the two Mini SuperDuos in step 8 **(figure 19)**. Pick up a 15º, an 11º, and a 15º, and sew through the Beam. Continue the three-bead pattern to the end, alternating the beads you sew through. Secure the last top hole of the protruding bead with a 15º. Complete the other side. This double layer makes the piece stiffen a little.

15. Add a clasp: Sew through a lower outer hole of an end Beam, pick up one or two 11ºs and a clasp loop, and sew back through the 11ºs and the Beam. Repeat this step to attach the remaining loop of the clasp **(figure 20)**. Retrace the thread path through the clasp connections, and end the working thread. Using the tail, repeat this step on the other end of the bracelet to secure the other half of the clasp. End the thread.

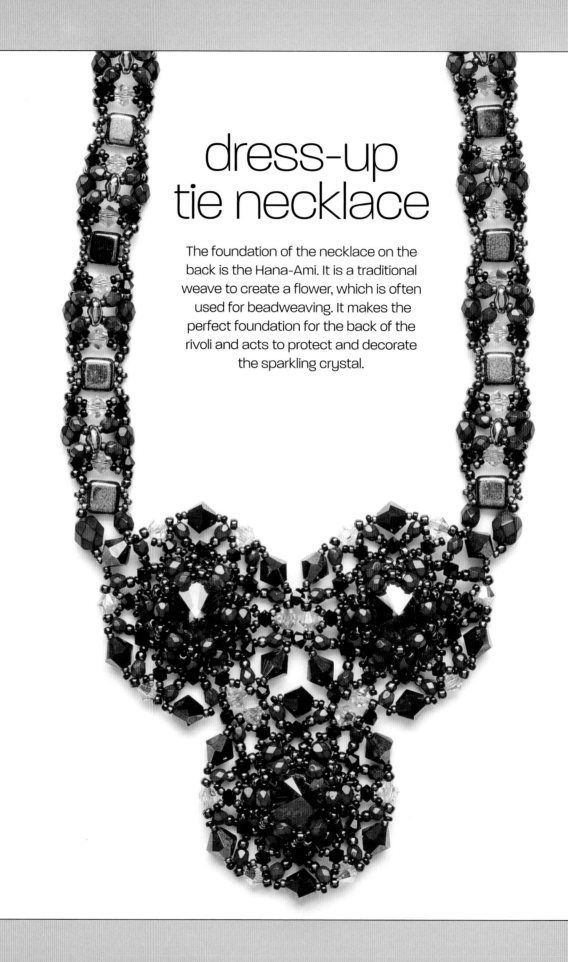

dress-up
tie necklace

The foundation of the necklace on the back is the Hana-Ami. It is a traditional weave to create a flower, which is often used for beadweaving. It makes the perfect foundation for the back of the rivoli and acts to protect and decorate the sparkling crystal.

Supplies

- **3** 14mm Swarovski rivolis (1122)
- **18** 6mm bicone crystals
- **4** 6mm fire-polished beads (optional)
- **38** 4mm fire-polished beads
- **30** 4mm bicone crystals
- **72** 3mm fire-polished beads
- **90** 3mm bicone crystals
- **24** SuperDuos
- **24** Tile beads
- 11º seed beads: 10g color A, 10g color B
- 15º seed bead: 7g color A, 5g color B
- Scissors
- Beading needles, size 12
- Fireline, 6-lb. test, or thread of your choice
- Two-hole clasp

MAKE THE NECKLACE

1. Thread a needle on about 2 yd. (1.8m) of thread, leaving a 6-in. (15cm) tail.

2. You will create the back side of the bezel first: Pick up six color A 11º seed beads, and sew through the beads again to form a ring. Tie a knot where the tail and working thread meet. Exit the 11º beyond the knot.

3. Start the petal pattern. Pick up a color A 15º seed bead, a color A 11º, a 3mm fire-polished bead, an A 11º, a 4mm fire-polished bead, an A 11º, a 3mm fire-polished, an A 11º, and an A 15º, and sew through the 11º you originally exited from the opposite side. Sew through the beadwork to exit the next 11º in the center ring (**figure 1**).

4. Pick up an A 15º, an A 11º, a 3mm fire-polished, an A 11º, a 4mm fire-polished, and an A 11º, and sew through the 3mm fire-polished on the side of the first petal. Continue to sew through the next beads in that leg and the 11º that you originally exited, and continue through the next 11º in the center ring (**figure 2**).

5. Repeat step 4 three more times (**figure 3**). On the fifth spoke of the wheel, sew through the beadwork to exit the 3mm fire-polished on the first spoke (**figure 4**).

6. The final set of beads are an A 11º, 4mm fire-polished, and an A 11º. This forms the back of the bezel (**figure 5**). Sew through the beadwork to exit an 11º after the 4mm fire-polished along the outer ring.

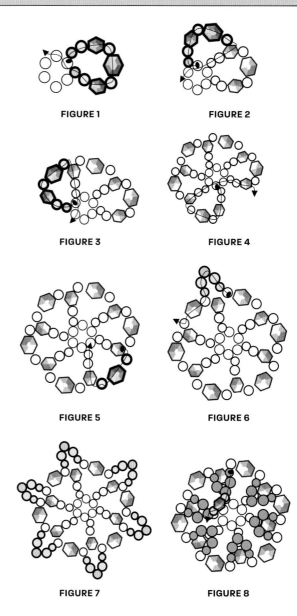

FIGURE 1

FIGURE 2

FIGURE 3

FIGURE 4

FIGURE 5

FIGURE 6

FIGURE 7

FIGURE 8

7. Next, create the bezel to capture the rivoli. This will start with a series of independent loops off the edge beads of the motif. Pick up an A 15º, an A 11º, a color B 11º seed bead, an A 11º, and an A 15º. Note the 11º's used at this point are best in two colors. Sew through the next A 11º, 4mm fire-polished, and A 11º (**figure 6**). Repeat the loop pattern, and continue around to create all six loops (**figure 7**).

8. Sew through the beadwork to exit the center B 11º just added on the loops, and connect each of the loops, folding them to the inside: Pick up an A 15º, a 3mm fire-polished, and an A 15º for the connection (**figure 8**). Sew through the next B 11º, and repeat around.

When you have connected all the loops, add the rivoli before you pull tight. Reinforce by sewing through all the beads in the inner circle encasing the rivoli. Sew through the beadwork to exit the 4mm fire-polished along the outer edge (figure 9).

9. Pick up an A 15º, an A 11º, a 3mm bicone crystal, an A 11º, and an A 15º. Sew through the next 4mm fire-polished. Repeat to complete the round (figure 10). Sew through the beadwork to exit a 3mm crystal added in this step.

10. Pick up an A 15º, a B 11º, a 3mm fire-polished, an A 11º, a 4mm crystal, an A 11º, a 3mm fire-polished, a B 11º, and an A 15º, and sew through the next 3mm crystal (figure 11). Repeat to complete the round, and exit a 4mm fire-polished in the middle of the wheel.

11. Next, fill the space between the 4mm fire-polished and 4mm crystals: Pick up an A 15º, a B 15º, a 3mm crystal, a B 15º, and an A 15º, and sew through the opposite 4mm. Pick up the same pattern of beads on the other side of the 3mm crystal to create an "X" (figure 12). Pull tight; there will be a slight puckering at this part. Repeat around (figure 13).

12. Back stitch from the 3mm fire-polished on the left side of the gap of an arm to the 3mm fire-polished on the right side of the next arm heading counter-clockwise with a combination of an A 15º, a B 15º, a 6mm crystal, a B 15º, and an A 15º (figure 14). Repeat to complete the round and end the threads.

13. Work as in steps 1–12 to make a second component.

14. Attach a comfortable length of thread to one of the components and sew through the beadwork to exit an 11º after a 4mm crystal. Connect the two components using a 3mm crystal on either side of the 11º, 4mm crystal, and 11º.

hint **You may complete the neck chain with a combination of beads, allowing them to curve by alternating sizes on the inside and outside edge. To achieve the curve, use a couple of 6mm fire-polished on the outside and 3mm fire-polished in the inside for a couple sections, and then switch to 4mms for several sections. You could also use seed beads; play with it a little to fit your neck.**

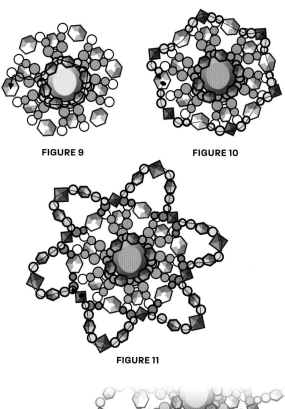

FIGURE 9   **FIGURE 10**

FIGURE 11

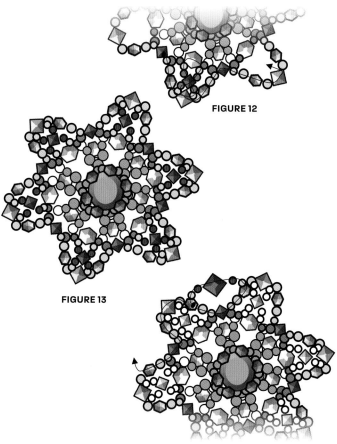

FIGURE 12

FIGURE 13

FIGURE 14

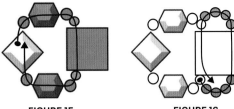

FIGURE 15

FIGURE 16

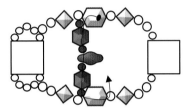

FIGURE 17

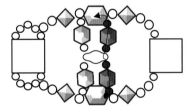

FIGURE 18

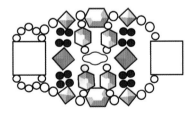

FIGURE 19

FIGURE 20

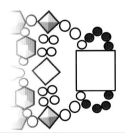

FIGURE 21

15. Attach a comfortable length of thread to an outer component. The neckstrap connects to the component through a 6mm along the outer edge. Determine where you want the neckstrap to attach, and sew through the beads to exit that 6mm crystal, referring to the photo on p. 104 for placement. Start the chain with a right-angle weave section. Pick up an A 11º, a 4mm fire-polished, an A 11º, an A 15º, a Tile bead, an A 15º, an A 11º, a 4mm fire-polished, and an A 11º, and sew through the 6mm again in the same direction **(figure 15)**. Continue through the next six beads to exit the A 15º after the Tile.

16. Continue to build the chain from the Tile. Pick up four A 15ºs, and sew through the available hole in the Tile. Pick up four A 15ºs, and sew through the A 15º and the first hole of the Tile **(figure 16)**. Sew through the beadwork to exit a 15º after the second Tile hole.

17. Pick up a B 11º, an A 11º, a 3mm crystal, an A 11º, a 4mm fire-polished, an A 11º, a 3mm crystal, an A 11º, a B 11º, an A 15º, a Tile, an A 15º, a B 11º, an A 11º, a 3mm crystal, an A 11º, a 4mm fire-polished, an A 11º, a 3mm crystal, an A 11º, and a B 11º, and sew through the 15º, Tile, and 15º your thread exited at the start of this step **(figure 17)**. These long loop of beads will build the chain. Sew all around to reinforce and exit the 4mm fire-polished.

18. Connect the 4mm fire-polished to the opposite 4mm fire-polished on the loop of beads: Pick up a 15º, a 3mm fire-polished, a 15º, a SuperDuo, a 15º, a 3mm fire-polished, and a 15º, and sew through the 4mm fire-polished on the other side of the ring in the opposite direction **(figure 18)**.

19. Pick up a 15º, a 3mm fire-polished, and a 15º, and sew through the available hole of the SuperDuo. Pick up a 15º, a 3mm fire-polished, and a 15º, and sew through the outer ring fire-polished **(figure 19)**.

20. Exit the 3mm crystal on the long string of beads. Pick up two 15ºs, a 4mm crystal, and two 15ºs, and sew through the opposite 3mm crystal. Complete the "X" by picking up two 15ºs and sewing through the 4mm crystal and then two more 15ºs to exit the opposite side 3mm crystal **(figure 20)**. Repeat on the other side. Note the SuperDuo component raises up a little. Sew through the beadwork to exit the 15º after the end Tile.

21. Work as in step 16 to add four 15ºs on both sides of the Tile **(figure 21)**.

22. Repeat steps 17–21 to the desired length to hit at the top of your shoulder (about 4–8 sections).

23. The next section of chain uses Tiles and SuperDuos in a different combination of beads. Exit the edge Tile on the existing chain. Pick up a 15º, a B 11º, two 15ºs, a SuperDuo, two 15ºs, a B 11º, and a 15º, and sew through the original 15º, Tile, and 15º **(figure 22)**. Sew through the beadwork to exit the 15º after the SuperDuo.

24. Pick up two 15ºs, and sew through the available hole of the SuperDuo. Pick up two 15ºs, and sew through a 15º and a SuperDuo **(figure 23)**. Sew through the beadwork to exit a 15º after a SuperDuo.

25. Pick up a 15º, a B 11º, two 15ºs, a Tile, two 15ºs, a B 11º, and a 15º, and sew through the first 15º and SuperDuo **(figure 24)**. Sew through the beadwork to exit a 15º beyond the added Tile.

26. Work as in step 16 to add 15ºs around the Tile **(figure 25)**.

27. Repeat step 23–26 to the desired length (about 2–4 sections on average to the back of the neck).

28. Exit the last SuperDuo to attach a clasp. Pick up three 11ºs and one half of the clasp, and pass back through the last 11º. Pick up two more 11ºs, and pass back through the 15º, SuperDuo, and 15º to reinforce **(figure 26)**. Repeat on the other end of the bracelet.

advanced

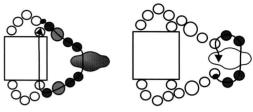

FIGURE 22   **FIGURE 23**

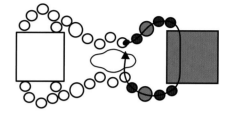

FIGURE 24

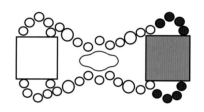

FIGURE 25

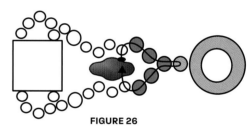

FIGURE 26

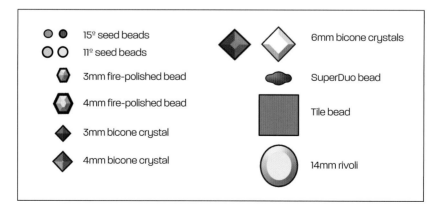

15º seed beads

11º seed beads

3mm fire-polished bead

4mm fire-polished bead

3mm bicone crystal

4mm bicone crystal

6mm bicone crystals

SuperDuo bead

Tile bead

14mm rivoli

gallery

FROM THE AUTHOR

Acknowledgments

Writing acknowledgments is difficult. I don't want to miss anyone. So many people have influenced my beading and inspired me over the years. Of course, my mother and her love for jewelry started it all. I have fond memories of exploring my mother's jewelry box. I admired the pieces and asked about them as a child. That curiosity and love for jewelry continued. The passion shared with my mother led to a lifetime of artistic discovery.

Family and many friends continued to inspire my passion and encouraged me to share with others. I am so grateful for their encouragement, and I love to share my enthusiasm. I found so much joy in the whole process, it has defined my life. I love building jewelry in intriguing ways and hope to inspire you as well.

My husband Jack encouraged me for the entire year of work. He would ask daily what I was going to do today. My reply of "the book" would result in a deep chuckle and comment of "oh, something different." He passed not long after the cover was released. He would have loved seeing the book.

I am now fortunate to work with several local bead stores in Florida who have encouraged, influenced, and challenged me to continue to create more fun and unique designs. The Beaded Garden, owned by Pamela Garbig, is near The Villages, Florida and closest to my home and heart. My friend Pamela encouraged me to write this book. Without her influence, this book may never have happened.

My work with the Starman Trendsetter team and Nichole Starman over the course of many years has also influenced my work. I appreciate their support and encouragement.

Several friends and exceptional students have helped with testing patterns, proofing, and contributing samples. Terri Perez Grego, Sandy Taylor, Becky Carr, and Rene Chambers have all taken a notable part of this process and I am grateful. Luella Duncan Frank deserves special mention as the color queen. She picked the colors and beads, and made the samples to match the top. Luella also made several other samples, and tested even more of the projects.

My publisher, Kalmbach Books, notably Dianne Wheeler and Erica Barse, have helped me along and encouraged me to realize my dream.

But most of all, my thanks go to my many students. So many of my students have encouraged me to write this book and supported me in my beading classes. It is for the love of beading, the desire to learn, and the passion to share, that this book has come to pass. Bead Happy.

About the Author

Marcia has worked with beads since her hippie years—a very long time ago. She has taught a variety of bead pieces at national, regional, and local levels for over 20 years while traveling for work as a financial manager. After retirement from the financial world in 2008, Marcia says she changed from being a "bean" counter to a "bead" counter. Her publications include numerous articles in many bead and mixed medial publications, including *Bead&Button*, *Beadwork*, *Jewelry Crafts*, *Perlen Posie*, *Bead Jewellery Magazine* (UK), *Expressions*, and *Belle Armoire*. Marcia taught at various national conventions, including Art Continuum, Celebrate Art, Bead Fest, and at The Bead&Button Show every year since 2005. She also teaches at regional retreats and at bead stores. Marcia loves to share her passion for beadwork with her students.

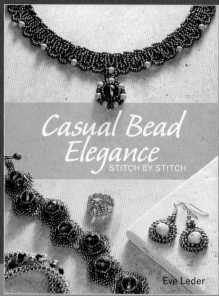